WHISPERS FROM THE HEART
A 30-Day Devotional for Authentic Living

GREG PAI

FIRST EDITION

Copyright © 2025 Gregory Pai
All rights reserved.
ISBN 979-8-9943883-0-3 (Hardcover)
ISBN 979-8-9943883-1-0 (Softcover)
ISBN 979-8-9943883-2-7 (eBook)

All rights reserved. This book may not be reproduced in whole or in part, stored in a retrieval system, or transmitted in any form or by any means—electronic, mechanical, or other—without written permission from the author,
except by a reviewer who may quote brief passages in a review.

Scripture quotations are taken from the Holy Bible, New Living Translation, copyright © 1996, 2004, 2015 by Tyndale House Foundation. Used by permission of Tyndale House Publishers, Carol Stream, Illinois 60188. All rights reserved.

Published by Voice of the Heart Books

*To those who are searching
for purpose, peace, and passion*

TABLE OF CONTENTS

INTRODUCTION 1

DAY 1 RECOGNIZING THE HIDDEN BATTLE 7

DAY 2 BLESSED TO BE A BLESSING 11

DAY 3 SYSTEMS OF SOCIETY THAT SHAPE US 15

DAY 4 THE WARRIOR'S AWAKENING 23

DAY 5 BUILDING ON SOLID GROUND 29

DAY 6 FINDING THE FATHER'S HEART 33

DAY 7 LEARNING, GOD'S WAY 39

DAY 8 BEYOND EMPTY RELIGION 43

DAY 9 FILTERING WHAT SHAPES YOU 47

DAY 10 GUARDING YOUR HEART IN A MEDIA WORLD 51

DAY 11 FINDING TRUTH IN A WORLD OF NOISE 55

DAY 12 MASTER, NOT MASTERED 59

DAY 13 BREAKING FREE FROM WORLDLY SYSTEMS 63

DAY 14 TRUE WEALTH IN GOD'S ECONOMY 67

DAY 15 CITIZENSHIP IN TWO KINGDOMS 71

DAY 16 BUILDING BRIDGES OF UNITY 75

DAY 17 FINDING TRUE SECURITY 79

Day 18 Wholeness in Body and Spirit 83

Day 19 Justice That Reflects God's Heart 87

Day 20 The Path of Peace 91

Day 21 Recognizing the Enemy's Arsenal 95

Day 22 Defending Your True Identity 99

Day 23 Standing Firm in God's Truth 103

Day 24 Keeping Your Spiritual Fire Burning 107

Day 25 Awakening to Spiritual Warfare 111

Day 26 Finding Your God-Given Path 115

Day 27 Discovering Your God Given Purpose 121

Day 28 Peace That Stands on Truth 125

Day 29 Fueling Your Spiritual Fire 129

Day 30 Shining as Light in the Darkness 133

Closing Prayer 139

About the Author 141

Continue the Journey 143

In The Beginning

INTRODUCTION

WHISPERS

Welcome to *Whispers from the Heart*, a transformative 30-day spiritual cleanse designed to guide you—throughout the year and over the course of your life—through the battle for your purpose, peace, and passion.

This devotional is designed to stand completely on its own, but also serves as a spiritual companion to *Voice of the Heart: The Battle for Your Purpose, Peace, and Passion* and the broader Voice of the Heart Collection. Each day's reading corresponds directly to a chapter from the main work, allowing you to journey through both books side by side for deeper exploration.

Through these pages, you will learn to recognize the unseen conflict around you, understand the systems that shape your thinking, and reclaim the abundant life God intended.

BATTLEFIELD WISDOM

This devotional follows a strategic battle plan, addressing different fronts of the spiritual war we face daily. The journey progresses deliberately:

- Days 1-4: Recognizing the unseen spiritual conflict at work in your life

- Days 5-20: Understanding the worldly systems designed to shape your thinking and behavior
- Days 21-25: Identifying and countering specific weapons used against your purpose, peace, and passion
- Days 26-30: Reclaiming your authentic identity and integrating these elements for maximum kingdom impact

Each devotional provides a complete spiritual battle plan with proven elements: Scripture memorization for embedding truth in your heart, biblical insights that illuminate both ancient wisdom and modern challenges, reflection questions that develop spiritual discernment, and practical application steps that transform knowledge into action.

Frontline Focus

Our modern battlefield includes unprecedented challenges unknown to previous generations—digital distractions that fragment attention, algorithms that shape beliefs without our awareness, and a culture that systematically disconnects us from God's design. This devotional addresses these contemporary challenges directly, offering spiritual strategies relevant to the complex world we navigate daily. The principles are timeless, but their application speaks directly to the unique spiritual warfare of our digital age.

Introduction

WARRIOR STRUCTURE

Each day's devotional equips you with:
- **Memory Verse** – Scripture to memorize as spiritual ammunition against the enemy's attacks
- **Today's Theme** – The central truth for the day
- **Battlefield Wisdom** – Biblical insights connecting Scripture to spiritual warfare
- **Frontline Focus** – Application to contemporary cultural challenges
- **Warrior Reflection** – Questions for theological understanding and personal application
- **Meditation Scripture** – An additional verse to deepen your perspective
- **Prayer** – A Trinitarian conversation addressing Father, Son, and Holy Spirit
- **Battle Strategy** – Three-tiered application options from simple first steps to advanced warrior challenges

HOW TO USE THIS DEVOTIONAL

This devotional isn't meant to be read once and shelved. It's designed as a spiritual cleanse you return to—monthly, seasonally, or whenever the world gets too loud.

Why? Because the enemy doesn't stop. The noise doesn't fade. The systems that shape your thinking keep working whether you're aware of them or not. Each time you journey through these 30 days, you'll see what you couldn't see before—and with each pass, the enemy's grip weakens while your discernment sharpens.

Consider returning to Day 1:

- **Monthly** — during seasons of intense spiritual battle
- **Quarterly** — to realign with each new season of life
- **Annually** — as a spiritual reset for the new year
- **In transition** — whenever circumstances shift and you need to hear God's voice again

You are not the same person you were last time. Let the same words meet the new you.

Whispers from the Heart can be used in two ways:

AS A STANDALONE JOURNEY:

If you do not have the companion book, *Voice of the Heart*, this devotional is designed to stand completely on its own and in fact, shares the same framework. Each day provides everything you need for meaningful reflection, prayer, and growth.

AS A COMPANION STUDY:

If you have access to Voice of the Heart, read each day's devotional alongside the corresponding chapter. This approach offers the richest experience, allowing you to explore the full depth of each topic while grounding it in daily spiritual practice.

Introduction

WARRIOR PREPARATION

Before beginning Day 1, take time to assess your current spiritual condition:
- Where do you sense your purpose, peace, or passion under attack?
- Which worldly systems most strongly influence your thinking?
- What specific truth are you seeking through this journey?

Write these reflections down and revisit them as you progress to track your transformation.

PRAYER

Heavenly Father, Creator, and Sovereign Lord, I acknowledge that You have designed me with purpose, equipped me for peace, and filled me with potential for passion. Lord Jesus, thank You for the victory You've already secured on the cross—making this battle not about winning but about claiming ground that is already mine. Holy Spirit, awaken the warrior within me through this devotional journey, sharpening my discernment and strengthening my resolve to stand firm in God's truth. Prepare my heart for transformation as I begin this 30-day journey. Amen.

Battle Strategy

First Step
Create a dedicated space and time for your daily devotional practice. Gather your Bible, a journal, and prepare this sacred appointment with God—ideally the same time each day for maximum impact.

Going Deeper
Begin a "Battle Journal" where you'll document insights, questions, and evidence of God's work throughout this 30-day journey. Include a "Before" assessment of where you currently stand in your purpose, peace, and passion.

Warrior Challenge
Invite a trusted friend to join you on this 30-day journey. Commit to weekly check-ins where you'll share discoveries, challenges, and pray specifically for each other's areas of spiritual warfare. Two warriors standing together greatly increase their effectiveness in battle.

Day 1
Recognizing the Hidden Battle

Seeing the Unseen Conflict
Voice of the Heart Reference: Chapter 1: A Different Kind of War

> *"For we are not fighting against flesh-and-blood enemies, but against evil rulers and authorities of the unseen world, against mighty powers in this dark world, and against evil spirits in the heavenly places." –Ephesians 6:12*

Today's Theme

Have you ever felt like something was working against you even when things seemed normal on the surface? That moment when you realize there's more happening than meets the eye is like what Paul describes in Ephesians. He reminds us that our real battles aren't just the everyday problems we can see, but a deeper spiritual conflict that affects everything in our lives.

Battlefield Wisdom

In Kenya, the author had a moment of clarity while photographing a lone Acacia tree. Something about that tree—standing strong despite harsh conditions—opened his eyes to a truth he'd felt but couldn't name: there's an invisible battle happening for our hearts and souls. This battle targets three vital parts of who we are: our purpose (who God made us to be), our peace (our connection to truth), and our passion (our love-fueled energy).

The Bible confirms this reality repeatedly. Jesus said in John 10:10, "The thief's purpose is to steal and kill and destroy. My purpose is to give them a rich and satisfying life." The enemy wants to disconnect us from the full, authentic life God intended. Like a snake in the garden that doesn't announce itself loudly, negative influences work quietly to pull us away from our true purpose, replacing God's truth with counterfeit substitutes.

FRONTLINE FOCUS

In today's digital landscape, this unseen battle takes new forms—social media algorithms that shape our identity, entertainment that subtly alters our values, and constant connectivity that fragments our attention. These modern forces don't announce themselves as enemies of our spiritual life, yet they often work powerfully against our divine purpose, replacing God's voice with a cacophony of competing influences.

WARRIOR REFLECTION

- **Understanding Truth:** When have you sensed something working against God's purpose for your life?
- **Heart Application:** What specific areas of your purpose, peace, or passion seem under the most attack right now?

Day 1
Recognizing the Hidden Battle

MEDITATION SCRIPTURE

> "Stay alert! Watch out for your great enemy, the devil. He prowls around like a roaring lion, looking for someone to devour. Stand firm against him, and be strong in your faith."
> –1 Peter 5:8-9

PRAYER

Father God, open my eyes to see the unseen battles in my life. Lord Jesus, help me recognize when something is trying to pull me away from the purpose You died to preserve. Holy Spirit, give me discernment to stand firm in my faith when attacks come. Thank You for fighting for me and promising that greater is He who is in me than he who is in the world. Amen.

BATTLE STRATEGY

FIRST STEP

Today, pause three times to assess what's influencing your thoughts and feelings. Each time, ask: "Is this pulling me toward God's purpose or away from it?"

GOING DEEPER

For the next three days, keep a small journal noting patterns of when you feel most attacked in your purpose, peace, or passion.

WARRIOR CHALLENGE

Share what you're learning about spiritual warfare with one trusted friend, asking them to be your prayer partner in recognizing these attacks.

NOTES:

Day 2
Blessed to be a Blessing

Discovering Mutual Strength Through Selfless Help

Voice of the Heart Reference: Chapter 2: A Different Kind of Book

"And God will generously provide all you need. Then you will always have everything you need and plenty left over to share with others."
—2 Corinthians 9:8

Today's Theme

God's promise to Abraham reveals a pattern that runs throughout Scripture: God blesses us so that we can bless others. This "blessed to be a blessing" principle shows that God's gifts are never meant to end with us. When God pours His goodness into our lives, it's designed to flow through us to benefit others.

Battlefield Wisdom

We often think we face a forced choice: either focus on helping ourselves or focus on helping others. This thinking creates a false divide that leaves us either selfishly focused on our own needs or burnt out from ignoring them while serving others. But God's way is neither selfish nor self-sacrificing—it's what we might call "selfless help."

Selfless help happens when meeting your needs and others' needs align perfectly. Think about teaching someone a skill you've mastered. As you teach, the learner gains knowledge while your own understanding deepens. Or consider how Jesus fed the 5,000—when the disciples gave what little they had, they didn't go hungry. Instead, there was abundance for everyone! This is the kingdom principle at work: when we give from what God has given us, everyone receives blessing.

FRONTLINE FOCUS

Our consumption-driven culture has trained us to be endpoints rather than channels. Marketing constantly tells us to accumulate, upgrade, and stockpile resources exclusively for ourselves. This stands in direct opposition to God's design for resources to flow through us, creating prosperity networks rather than prosperity islands.

WARRIOR REFLECTION

- **Understanding Truth:** How does God's "blessed to be a blessing" principle challenge our cultural understanding of success and prosperity?
- **Heart Application:** In what area of your life might God be calling you to be a channel rather than just a container of His blessing?

Day 2
Blessed to be a Blessing

MEDITATION SCRIPTURE

"And I have been a constant example of how you can help those in need by working hard. You should remember the words of the Lord Jesus: 'It is more blessed to give than to receive.'"
—Acts 20:35

PRAYER

Heavenly Father, You are the ultimate giver, the source of every blessing. Thank You for Your generous nature and for including me in Your divine flow of goodness. Lord Jesus, You modeled selfless giving, emptying Yourself for our benefit while experiencing the joy that comes through sacrifice. Holy Spirit, guide me to recognize opportunities to be a channel of blessing to others. Amen.

BATTLE STRATEGY

FIRST STEP

Identify one blessing God has given you (a talent, resource, or experience) and find one specific way to share it this week that serves others while also filling your own cup.

GOING DEEPER

For the next seven days, practice "blessing awareness" by ending each day identifying: (1) one way God blessed you, and (2) one way you channeled God's blessing to someone else.

WARRIOR CHALLENGE

Create a "blessing flow plan" for one significant resource in your life (time, money, skills, home, etc.). Redesign how you use this resource so it intentionally blesses others while still meeting your needs.

NOTES:

___

___

___

___

___

___

___

___

___

Day 3
Systems of Society That Shape Us

Recognizing Worldly Influences
Voice of the Heart Reference: Chapter 3: Infiltration

"Don't copy the behavior and customs of this world, but let God transform you into a new person by changing the way you think. Then you will learn to know God's will for you, which is good and pleasing and perfect." —Romans 12:2

Today's Theme

Paul's warning not to "conform to the pattern of this world" shows remarkable insight. He understood that the world has patterns—systems and structures—designed to shape us into its image rather than God's. These patterns don't just suggest; they actively mold us, often without our awareness.

Battlefield Wisdom

Just as a tree has different parts—roots, trunk, branches, and fruit—the systems around us form a living structure that shapes who we become. Our foundation comes from family, education, and religious training. Our information flows through media, news, and technology.

Our connections form through economic, governmental, and social systems. And our legacy emerges through health, justice, and security systems.

Each of these systems was originally designed for good but can be twisted to pull us away from God's purposes. Jesus understood this when He prayed in John 17:15-16, "I'm not asking you to take them out of the world, but to keep them safe from the evil one. They do not belong to this world any more than I do." Christ calls us to live in these systems while being guided by different values—kingdom values that often run counter to worldly patterns.

THE ARCHITECTURE OF INFILTRATION

The enemy's strategy isn't random. It's systematic—and it follows a pattern as old as creation itself.

Think of a tree. Every tree has four parts: roots that anchor it and draw nutrients from the soil, a trunk that channels resources and information, branches that extend outward into the world, and fruit that represents its ultimate output and legacy. To be clear, this isn't the "fruit of the Spirit" Paul describes in Galatians—personal virtues like love and peace. This is the fruit of Genesis: God's command to "be fruitful and multiply." These systems determine whether humanity can fulfill that mandate—or whether the cycle of human flourishing is disrupted at its source.

The enemy has infiltrated each level:

THE ROOTS
FOUNDATIONAL SYSTEMS (DAYS 5-8)

Family, education, and religion form the soil of our identity—where we first learn who we are, what to believe, and what matters. God established family as humanity's first institution, commanded parents to teach His ways to their children, and

Day 3
Systems of Society That Shape Us

designed worship to anchor us in truth. When the enemy corrupts the roots, he attacks identity itself. A child who doesn't know they bear God's image cannot understand whose they are. A foundation cracked at the source compromises everything built upon it. The enemy's first question to humanity wasn't a command—it was an identity assault: "Did God really say...?"

THE TRUNK
INFORMATION SYSTEMS (DAYS 9-12)

Media, news, and technology act as the trunk—controlling what information flows to us and how we interpret reality. God designed us to receive and transmit truth; His Word was meant to be the filter through which we understand everything else. A poisoned trunk doesn't just weaken the tree—it corrupts every message that passes through it. When the enemy controls the flow of information, he doesn't need to destroy truth; he only needs to drown it in noise. If you cannot discern God's voice from the world's, you cannot recognize the lies crafted specifically for you.

THE BRANCHES
SOCIAL & ECONOMIC SYSTEMS (DAYS 13-17)

Economics, government, and social structures extend outward like branches, shaping how we interact with the world and how far our influence can reach. God designed work to be fruitful, community to be covenantal, and governance to protect human flourishing. When the enemy corrupts the branches, he redirects our energy toward purposes that serve his kingdom instead of God's. Our reach becomes constrained. Our resources get consumed. Our relationships turn transactional. The branches still look alive, but they bear the enemy's agenda—not the Father's.

THE FRUIT
SECURITY & LEGACY SYSTEMS (DAYS 18-20)

Healthcare, justice, and military systems represent the fruit—humanity's capacity to fulfill God's command to *"be fruitful and multiply."* These aren't outputs; they're the conditions that determine whether the next generation takes root at all. Healthcare affects fertility, childbearing, and survival. Justice determines whether families can form and thrive in safety. Military decides whether there's peace for humanity to flourish—or war that decimates generations before they begin. When these systems are corrupted, the enemy doesn't just hinder human flourishing—he disrupts the divine mandate at its source.

Understanding this architecture changes everything. You're not fighting random battles. You're dismantling a carefully constructed system—root, trunk, branch, and fruit.

Over Days 5 through 20, we'll examine each level. But remember: the goal isn't just to understand the tree. It's to plant a new one.

FRONTLINE FOCUS

The enemy's infiltration of these systems isn't new—it began in Eden. The serpent's first attack targeted the root (twisting God's word), corrupted the trunk (distorting Eve's understanding), extended through the branches (drawing Adam into participation), and struck at the fruit (threatening humanity's ability to multiply in God's image). The tactics haven't changed. What has changed is the interconnectedness.

These systems don't operate in isolation—they form a web by design. Family shapes what education reinforces. Media amplifies what government permits. Economics

Day 3
Systems of Society That Shape Us

constrains what healthcare provides. Each thread strengthens the others, creating a fabric increasingly difficult to escape. Today's digital ecosystem hasn't introduced new devices; the enemy's playbook remains ancient. But technology has exponentially heightened the burden on our human capacity to recognize deception, resist manipulation, and defend our hearts. The battlefield is the same. The intensity is unprecedented.

WARRIOR REFLECTION

- **Understanding Truth:** How does understanding systems help explain why simply trying harder often fails to produce lasting spiritual growth?
- **Heart Application:** Which worldly system or pattern do you find most challenging to your faith right now?

MEDITATION SCRIPTURE

"Don't let anyone capture you with empty philosophies and high-sounding nonsense that come from human thinking and from the spiritual powers of this world, rather than from Christ."
—Colossians 2:8

Prayer

Heavenly Father, You designed the original systems of creation to work in perfect harmony. I ask for wisdom to recognize when these systems have been corrupted. Lord Jesus, You lived within worldly systems yet remained perfectly aligned with the Father's will. Holy Spirit, open my eyes to see the invisible patterns that shape me and transform my mind to recognize and resist worldly influences. Amen.

Battle Strategy

First Step

Choose one area of influence (media, social groups, education, etc.) and examine it prayerfully today. Ask: "How is this shaping my values? Does it align with God's Word?"

Going Deeper

Create a "system awareness map" by listing the key systems that influence you daily. For each one, identify one way it pulls you toward God's kingdom and one way it pulls you away.

Warrior Challenge

Form a small group to study how a specific system (education, media, economics, etc.) shapes Christian formation. Meet weekly for a month to develop practical strategies to live counter-culturally.

Day 3
Systems of Society That Shape Us

NOTES:

Day 4
The Warrior's Awakening

Finding Your Warrior Spirit
Voice of the Heart Reference:
Chapter 4: Awakening the Warrior in You

"No, despite all these things, overwhelming victory is ours through Christ, who loved us."
—Romans 8:37

Today's Theme

Paul's reminder to Timothy speaks directly to our spiritual identity. God hasn't created us to be victims, paralyzed by fear and oppressed by circumstances. Instead, He's equipped us with power, love, and self-discipline—the essential qualities of a spiritual warrior ready to stand firm in faith.

Battlefield Wisdom

Our journey with Christ follows a path of transformation through three distinct stages. Many begin as victims—unaware of the spiritual battle, easily shaped by the world's systems, and believing they have no power to change their circumstances.

Some progress to become soldiers. This is where many Christians get stuck. Soldiers recognize there's a battle. They've woken up to the reality that something is wrong. But here's the danger: soldiers often fight for the wrong side without realizing it. They enforce the very systems that limit them and others—perhaps by measuring success the world's way while adding Christian language, or by using spiritual authority to control rather than liberate.

But God calls us to become warriors—those who see clearly, stand firmly, and fight effectively for kingdom purposes. Warriors don't just recognize the battle; they understand who the real enemy is and refuse to become enforcers of oppressive systems, even religious ones.

David modeled this warrior spirit. When facing Goliath, he declared in 1 Samuel 17:45, "You come to me with sword, spear, and javelin, but I come to you in the name of the LORD of Heaven's Armies." His strength came not from military training but from identity in God. Similarly, our warrior spirit emerges through embracing who we are in Christ—beloved children clothed in His armor and authority, fighting with God rather than for systems that oppose Him.

⚔ THE ULTIMATE TRANSFORMATION
WHEN SAUL BECAME PAUL

No one illustrates the three stages better than Saul of Tarsus.

Saul began as a victim. He was a Jew living under Roman occupation—his people oppressed, their land colonized, their freedoms restricted by a foreign empire. Like all victims, he carried the weight of forces beyond his control shaping his identity and limiting his possibilities.

Day 4
The Warrior's Awakening

But Saul didn't stay passive. He became a soldier. Educated under the great teacher Gamaliel, he rose as a Pharisee—zealous, disciplined, and absolutely convinced he was fighting for God. In his own words: "I was so zealous that I harshly persecuted the church. And as for righteousness, I obeyed the law without fault" (Philippians 3:6).

Here's what soldiers do: they take their victim pain and channel it into enforcement. Saul couldn't overthrow Rome, but he could police his own people. He couldn't control the empire, but he could control who belonged and who didn't. He imprisoned believers. He approved of Stephen's execution. He breathed "murderous threats" against the early church (Acts 9:1)—all while believing he defended God's truth.

Saul was the perfect soldier. And he was completely wrong.

Then came Damascus. A blinding light. A voice: "Saul, Saul, why are you persecuting me?" (Acts 9:4).

In that moment, Saul discovered the devastating truth about soldiers: you can fight with absolute conviction and still be fighting against the very God you claim to serve.

The man who rose from that road was no longer a soldier. Paul the Warrior emerged—same fire, same zeal, same intensity—but now aligned with God's actual purposes. He would later write, "For we are not fighting against flesh-and-blood enemies, but against evil rulers and authorities of the unseen world" (Ephesians 6:12).

Paul never lost his fight. He lost his blindness.

Here's the uncomfortable truth: most of us, if we're fortunate, are Saul. We've moved beyond victim. We're no longer asleep. We see that something is wrong, and we're fighting—maybe fiercely. But are we fighting the right battle? Or have we channeled our pain into policing others and enforcing systems that feel righteous but miss God's heart entirely?

Being Saul isn't failure. It's progress. Victims don't even know there's a war. Saul knew—he just needed his eyes opened.

> The good news? Saul became Paul. And so can you.
> Are you ready for your Damascus moment?

FRONTLINE FOCUS

In an age where victimhood is often celebrated and personal responsibility diminished, embracing your warrior identity is profoundly countercultural. Social media platforms often reward displays of weakness and vulnerability while offering little accountability for growth or transformation. The warrior path calls us to a different story—one where challenges become opportunities for God's power to be displayed through our weakness.

WARRIOR REFLECTION

- **Understanding Truth:** What is the difference between fighting in your own strength versus fighting in God's strength?
- **Heart Application:** Where in your life are you still functioning as a victim rather than as a warrior?
- **Soldier Check:** Like Saul before Damascus, where might your own pain or frustration be driving you to enforce systems—religious, cultural, societal, or otherwise—rather than liberate people from them?

MEDITATION SCRIPTURE

> *"For God has not given us a spirit of fear and timidity, but of power, love, and self-discipline."*
> *—2 Timothy 1:7*

Day 4
The Warrior's Awakening

Prayer

Heavenly Father, thank You for not giving me a spirit of fear but equipping me with power, love, and a sound mind. Lord Jesus, You demonstrated perfect warrior strength by conquering sin and death not through domination but through sacrificial love. Holy Spirit, awaken the warrior spirit within me—not to fight against people, but to stand against the spiritual forces that oppose God's purposes. Amen.

Battle Strategy

First Step

Identify one situation where you've felt powerless. Write down three ways you could approach it as a warrior rather than a victim, remembering you have God's power available to you.

Going Deeper

Create a "warrior identity" card with three biblical truths about who you are in Christ. Carry it with you and read it aloud when you find yourself slipping into victim mentality.

Warrior Challenge

Find someone who needs encouragement to move from victim to warrior. Share your journey and pray together weekly for a month, celebrating steps of faith and courage you each take.

NOTES:

Day 5
Building on Solid Ground

Examining Your Foundation
*Voice of the Heart Reference: Chapter 5:
Foundational & Formative Systems*

"Anyone who listens to my teaching and follows it is wise, like a person who builds a house on solid rock." —Matthew 7:24

Today's Theme

Jesus's parable about building on rock versus sand reveals a profound truth: our foundation determines whether we stand or fall when storms come. Just as a house needs a solid foundation, our lives need the bedrock of Christ's teachings to weather life's challenges.

Battlefield Wisdom

Our early foundations matter tremendously. The family systems, educational experiences, and religious training we receive in our formative years shape how we see ourselves, others, and God. Like soil that affects what a garden can grow, these foundations influence everything that comes later. Some of us received rich, nurturing soil that supported healthy growth. Others faced rocky ground or shallow soil that made growth challenging.

The good news is that God specializes in helping things grow in difficult places. In 1 Corinthians 3:11, Paul declares, "For no one can lay any foundation other than the one we already have—Jesus Christ." No matter what foundation you started with, Christ offers Himself as the solid rock upon which you can rebuild. Like a tree that can grow through concrete, God's power can help us thrive despite challenging beginnings.

FRONTLINE FOCUS

Today's "foundation-less" culture promotes building life on shifting trends, fleeting emotions, and relativistic values. Social media influencers change their core beliefs with algorithmic winds, modeling a sand-based approach to life. Christ calls us to the countercultural practice of anchoring our identity, values, and decisions in His unchanging truth—a foundation that remains stable regardless of cultural shifts.

WARRIOR REFLECTION

- **Understanding Truth:** Why does Jesus emphasize both hearing AND practicing His words as the way to build a solid foundation?
- **Heart Application:** Which aspects of your early foundation need to be rebuilt on the solid rock of Christ?

Day 5
Building on Solid Ground

MEDITATION SCRIPTURE

> *"They are like trees planted along the riverbank, bearing fruit each season. Their leaves never wither, and they prosper in all they do."*
> —Psalm 1:3

PRAYER

Heavenly Father, You are the master architect who designed the blueprint for human flourishing. Lord Jesus, thank You for being the solid rock I can build my life upon. Holy Spirit, help me recognize where my early foundations were weak or distorted. Heal the places where faulty teaching or painful experiences have shaped my understanding, and root me deeply in God's truth so I can grow strong. Amen.

BATTLE STRATEGY

FIRST STEP

List three key beliefs about yourself or God that were formed in your early years. Compare each with Scripture to see if it aligns with God's truth.

GOING DEEPER

Create a "foundation assessment" by identifying one belief from your family system, one from your educational experience, and one from your religious training that needs realignment with Scripture.

WARRIOR CHALLENGE

Start a Bible study focusing on Jesus's teachings in the Sermon on the Mount (Matthew 5-7). Invite others to join you in examining how these teachings create a solid foundation for life.

NOTES:

Day 6
Finding the Father's Heart

Healing Family Patterns
Voice of the Heart Reference: Chapter 6: Family Dynamics

> "And I will be your Father, and you will be my sons and daughters, says the LORD Almighty."
> —2 Corinthians 6:18

Today's Theme

God describes Himself as "a father to the fatherless" because He understands how profoundly our family experiences shape us. Whether our earthly families were nurturing or hurtful, God promises to meet us in our deepest family wounds and provide the perfect love that human relationships often cannot.

Battlefield Wisdom

Our earliest relationships form the template for how we view ourselves, others, and God. The patterns we experience in family—whether love or neglect, acceptance, or rejection, truth or deception—create pathways in our hearts and minds that affect every future relationship. When these patterns are healthy, they prepare us to receive God's love.

When they're distorted, they can make trusting God difficult.

The beautiful promise of the gospel is that God can heal these patterns. In Romans 8:15, Paul writes, "So you have not received a spirit that makes you fearful slaves. Instead, you received God's Spirit when he adopted you as his own children. Now we call him, 'Abba, Father.'" Through Christ, we're adopted into God's family, giving us a new foundation that can transform our understanding of relationship.

FRONTLINE FOCUS

In an era of increasingly fractured families and redefined relationships, many struggle with father wounds, mother wounds, or the absence of healthy family models altogether. Digital "families" and online communities often substitute for genuine belonging but can't provide the secure attachment we need. God's offer of perfect fatherhood speaks powerfully to this contemporary crisis of identity and belonging.

WARRIOR REFLECTION

- **Understanding Truth:** How does God's perfect fatherhood heal the distortions we experience in human family relationships?
- **Heart Application:** What family pattern most needs God's healing touch in your life right now?

Day 6
Finding the Father's Heart

MEDITATION SCRIPTURE

*"Father to the fatherless, defender of widows—
this is God, whose dwelling is holy. God places the
lonely in families."* —Psalm 68:5-6a

PRAYER

Heavenly Father, thank You for adopting me into Your family through Christ. Where I've known rejection, help me receive Your perfect acceptance. Lord Jesus, You showed us the Father's heart in human form, revealing His true nature. Holy Spirit, heal the wounds that came from my earthly family experiences and transform the patterns that keep me from fully trusting You. Amen.

BATTLE STRATEGY

FIRST STEP

Identify one negative family pattern you've experienced or perpetuated. Write a prayer asking God to break this cycle in your life.

GOING DEEPER

Write a letter (that you don't need to send) to a family member who wounded you. Express your feelings honestly, then write God's perspective on the situation and His healing words to you.

WARRIOR CHALLENGE

Find a trusted mentor or counselor who can help you explore how your family dynamics have shaped your view of God. Meet regularly for three months to work through these patterns with prayer and Scripture.

Day 6
Finding the Father's Heart

NOTES:

Day 7
Learning, God's Way

Education That Liberates
Voice of the Heart Reference: Chapter 7: Education

"And you will know the truth, and the truth will set you free." —John 8:32

Today's Theme

Solomon reveals a profound truth: true education begins with reverence for God. While the world's educational systems focus on information, God's approach to learning starts with relationship. This "fear of the LORD" isn't about being afraid, but about recognizing God as the ultimate source of wisdom and the foundation of all true knowledge.

Battlefield Wisdom

God created us with natural curiosity and a love of discovery. Watch any young child learning to walk—they fall, get up, try again, driven by an innate desire to explore. Yet many educational experiences dampen this God-given curiosity, replacing wonder with standardized expectations and creative thinking with conformity.

Jesus modeled a radically different approach to teaching. He used questions, stories, and real-life situations to engage minds and hearts. Rather than filling passive listeners with facts, He invited active participation through parables that made people think. As Jesus often said, "Anyone with ears to hear should listen and understand!" (Matthew 11:15). Christ's method values our unique design, as Psalm 139:14 celebrates, "Thank you for making me so wonderfully complex! Your workmanship is marvelous—how well I know it."

FRONTLINE FOCUS

Today's information economy bombards us with more data than ever before, yet often leaves us less wise. Educational systems increasingly focus on marketable skills rather than character formation, creating knowledgeable people who lack wisdom. The digital age offers unprecedented access to information while simultaneously shortening attention spans needed for deep learning. God's educational approach offers a refreshing alternative—learning that transforms, not merely informs.

WARRIOR REFLECTION

- **Understanding Truth:** How is God's approach to education different from most formal educational systems you've experienced?
- **Heart Application:** How might approaching Scripture with childlike curiosity rather than just seeking information change your relationship with God?

Day 7
Learning, God's Way

MEDITATION SCRIPTURE

"All Scripture is inspired by God and is useful to teach us what is true and to make us realize what is wrong in our lives. It corrects us when we are wrong and teaches us to do what is right. God uses it to prepare and equip his people to do every good work." —2 Timothy 3:16-17

PRAYER

Heavenly Father, You are the source of all wisdom and knowledge. Thank You for creating me with natural curiosity and a desire to learn. Lord Jesus, You taught with authority yet made truth accessible through stories and examples. Help me learn as You taught. Holy Spirit, rekindle my love for learning about God and His world. Where educational experiences have dampened my curiosity, restore the wonder You designed me to have. Amen.

BATTLE STRATEGY

FIRST STEP

Choose a familiar Bible passage and read it with fresh eyes today, asking questions like a curious child: "I wonder why this happened?" or "What might this person have felt?"

GOING DEEPER

For one week, approach Scripture reading differently by using all your senses. As you read, imagine what you would see, hear, smell, taste, and touch if you were present in the story.

Warrior Challenge

Start a "wonder journal" documenting questions that arise in your spiritual journey. Instead of rushing to answers, spend time exploring each question with God, recording insights He provides through prayer, Scripture, and godly counsel.

NOTES:

Day 8
Beyond Empty Religion

Filling the Void
Voice of the Heart Reference: Chapter 8: Religion

"These people honor me with their lips, but their hearts are far from me." —Matthew 15:8

Today's Theme

When Jesus spoke to the Samaritan woman at the well, He transformed her understanding of worship. She was caught in a debate about the right place to worship, but Jesus shifted the focus to the heart of the worshiper. God isn't looking for perfect religious performance—He's seeking those who connect with Him authentically, from the heart.

Battlefield Wisdom

Religion at its worst becomes a system of rules without relationship—rituals performed to earn favor rather than expressions of love. Jesus repeatedly confronted this empty approach, telling the Pharisees in Matthew 23:27, "What sorrow awaits you teachers of religious law and you Pharisees. Hypocrites! For you are like whitewashed tombs—beautiful on the outside but filled on the inside with dead people's bones and all sorts of impurity." These religious leaders had mastered the external practices while missing the heart of faith.

God invites us into something profoundly different—an authentic relationship where we bring our real questions, doubts, and struggles. James 1:27 describes what pure religion looks like: "Pure and genuine religion in the sight of God the Father means caring for orphans and widows in their distress and refusing to let the world corrupt you." This is faith expressed through love and integrity, not just religious activities.

FRONTLINE FOCUS

In today's "spiritual but not religious" culture, many have rejected institutional faith altogether, often because they've experienced its empty forms without its transforming power. Social media spirituality offers personalized belief systems without accountability or community. Against this backdrop, authentic faith that combines deep conviction with genuine humility, theological substance with compassionate action, speaks powerfully to a world tired of religious performance.

WARRIOR REFLECTION

- **Understanding Truth:** What's the difference between relationship-based faith and rules-based religion according to Scripture?

Day 8
Beyond Empty Religion

- **Heart Application:** Where in your spiritual life have you been going through motions without heart engagement?

Meditation Scripture

"But the time is coming—indeed it's here now—when true worshipers will worship the Father in spirit and in truth. The Father is looking for those who will worship him that way." —John 4:23

Prayer

Heavenly Father, forgive me for times when I've substituted religious activity for authentic relationship with You. Lord Jesus, You confronted empty religion and modeled true connection with the Father. Help me follow Your example. Holy Spirit, draw me into genuine worship that springs from my heart. Free me from performance-based spirituality and lead me into the freedom of being fully known and fully loved. Amen.

Battle Strategy

First Step

Take five minutes today for an honest conversation with God about something you've been hesitant to discuss with Him. Remember that He already knows and welcomes your authenticity.

Going Deeper

Examine your spiritual practices this week. For each one, ask: "Am I doing this from genuine love for God or from obligation?" Adjust your approach based on your answers.

Warrior Challenge

Find someone who has been wounded by empty religion. Listen to their story without defensiveness, then share how Jesus also confronted religious systems that hurt rather than healed. Invite them to explore authentic faith with you.

NOTES:

Day 9
Filtering What Shapes You

Guarding Your Perception
Voice of the Heart Reference: Chapter 9: Influence & Control Systems

> *"but test everything that is said. Hold on to what is good. Stay away from every kind of evil."*
> —1 Thessalonians 5:21-22

Today's Theme

John's warning to "test the spirits" reminds us that not everything presenting itself as truth actually is. Like wearing tinted glasses that change how everything looks, the information we receive filters our perception of reality. God calls us to carefully examine what influences are shaping how we see the world.

Battlefield Wisdom

Just as a tree's trunk determines what nutrients flow from roots to branches, the information systems in our lives control what reaches our awareness. These "trunk" systems—media, news, technology—filter what we perceive as real, important, or meaningful. When these filters align with God's truth, they help us grow. When they distort reality, they can lead us away from God's purposes.

Jesus warned about this in Matthew 6:22-23, saying, "Your eye is like a lamp that provides light for your body. When your eye is healthy, your whole body is filled with light. But when your eye is unhealthy, your whole body is filled with darkness." What we allow into our minds shapes our entire life. Paul gives practical guidance in Philippians 4:8, urging us: "And now, dear brothers and sisters, one final thing. Fix your thoughts on what is true, and honorable, and right, and pure, and lovely, and admirable. Think about things that are excellent and worthy of praise." This verse offers a divine filter for evaluating what deserves our attention.

FRONTLINE FOCUS

Today's information ecosystem creates unprecedented challenges for discernment. Algorithms curate personalized reality tunnels, deepfakes blur the line between truth and fiction, and attention engineers design content to maximize engagement rather than understanding. In this environment, developing strong information filters isn't just helpful—it's essential for maintaining a Christ-centered worldview amid relentless distortion.

WARRIOR REFLECTION

- **Understanding Truth:** What criteria does Scripture give us for evaluating the information we consume?

- **Heart Application:** What information sources are shaping your reality, and filtering your perception?

Day 9
Filtering What Shapes You

MEDITATION SCRIPTURE

"Dear friends, do not believe everyone who claims to speak by the Spirit. You must test them to see if the spirit they have comes from God. For there are many false prophets in the world."
—1 John 4:1

PRAYER

Heavenly Father, You are the source of all truth in a world full of deception. Lord Jesus, You said "I am the truth," offering yourself as the standard by which all claims should be measured. Holy Spirit, sharpen my discernment to recognize what shapes my perception of reality. Help me test everything against God's Word, holding fast to what is true and rejecting what distorts. Give me wisdom to choose information sources that align with Your values. Amen.

BATTLE STRATEGY

FIRST STEP

Review your main sources of news and information today. For each one, ask: "Does this help me see the world more like Jesus does?"

GOING DEEPER

Practice the "five-minute pause" before sharing information this week. Take five minutes to verify claims, consider motivations, and pray about whether sharing serves God's purposes before posting or forwarding content.

WARRIOR CHALLENGE

Create a "media discernment group" with trusted believers. Meet monthly to discuss current information trends, evaluate media sources together, and hold each other accountable for consuming and sharing truth rather than distortion.

NOTES:

Day 10
Guarding Your Heart in a Media World
Finding Your True Identity
Voice of the Heart Reference: Chapter 10: Media & Entertainment

> *"And now, dear brothers and sisters, one final thing. Fix your thoughts on what is true, and honorable, and right, and pure, and lovely, and admirable. Think about things that are excellent and worthy of praise."* —Philippians 4:8

Today's Theme

Solomon's wisdom to "guard your heart" takes on new urgency in today's media-saturated world. What we watch, read, and listen to doesn't just entertain us—it shapes who we become. The heart Solomon mentions isn't just our emotions but the core of our identity, the source of our thoughts, feelings, and actions.

Battlefield Wisdom

Media and entertainment don't merely reflect culture—they actively create it. The average person spends more time consuming media than in conversation with family or in prayer with God. This massive influence subtly replaces our God-given identity with manufactured substitutes, telling us who we should be, what we should value, and how we should live.

Jesus warned about this struggle over our identity in Matthew 6:24, saying, "No one can serve two masters. For you will hate one and love the other; you will be devoted to one and despise the other." While He was speaking about money, the principle applies to media influence as well. We cannot serve both the image of success promoted by our entertainment culture and the kingdom values Jesus taught. Paul offers practical guidance in Romans 12:2, urging us: "Don't copy the behavior and customs of this world, but let God transform you into a new person by changing the way you think." This transformation happens as we intentionally choose what influences our thinking.

FRONTLINE FOCUS

Today's entertainment technologies create unprecedented immersive experiences designed to capture not just attention but identity. Streaming services that automatically play the next episode, social media feeds that deliver dopamine-triggering content, and virtual worlds that offer escapism combine to form powerful identity-shaping forces. These platforms aren't neutral—they're designed to transform us into ideal consumers rather than faithful disciples.

WARRIOR REFLECTION

- **Understanding Truth:** How does Scripture guide us to evaluate the entertainment we consume?

Day 10
Guarding Your Heart in a Media World

- **Heart Application:** What characters or personalities in media have influenced how you see yourself or what you value compared to your identity in Christ?

MEDITATION SCRIPTURE

"Guard your heart above all else, for it determines the course of your life." —Proverbs 4:23

PRAYER

Heavenly Father, You have given me a specific identity as Your beloved child. Lord Jesus, in You I find my true self, not in the images promoted by media and entertainment. Holy Spirit, help me guard my heart from influences that pull me away from Your truth. Show me where I've allowed entertainment to shape my identity more than Your Word. Give me wisdom to choose media that builds up rather than tears down the person You created me to be. Amen.

BATTLE STRATEGY

FIRST STEP

Take a media inventory today: Track how much time you spend with different forms of media and how each makes you feel afterward.

Going Deeper

Choose one form of media to either limit or eliminate this week, replacing that time with Scripture reading or prayer that reinforces your identity in Christ.

Warrior Challenge

Create a "media fast and feast" plan for one month: Identify media to eliminate (fast) and life-giving content to increase (feast). Share your plan with an accountability partner who will check in weekly on your progress.

NOTES:

Day 11
Finding Truth in a World of Noise

Discerning What's Real
Voice of the Heart Reference: Chapter 11: News & Information

"Only simpletons believe everything they're told! The prudent carefully consider their steps."
—Proverbs 14:15

Today's Theme

Solomon's contrast between the "simple" who believe anything and the "prudent" who carefully consider information speaks directly to our news-saturated world. With constant headlines, updates, and alerts competing for our attention, God calls us to be thoughtful consumers of information, not passive receivers of whatever comes our way.

Battlefield Wisdom

News and information systems don't just inform us—they shape how we see reality. Through selective reporting, emotional language, and constant urgency, they create a narrative about what matters and how we should respond. This isn't a new challenge. Even in biblical times, false reports spread quickly. When Joshua and Caleb returned from exploring the Promised Land, ten other spies spread fear through exaggerated reports, leading an entire generation astray.

Jesus taught us: "Look, I am sending you out as sheep among wolves. So be as shrewd as snakes and harmless as doves" (Matthew 10:16), combining discernment with purity of heart. Paul echoes this in 1 Thessalonians 5:21, instructing us: "but test everything that is said. Hold on to what is good." Rather than accepting or rejecting all information, we're called to carefully evaluate what we hear, comparing it with God's unchanging truth. This discernment allows us to find the peace Jesus promised.

FRONTLINE FOCUS

Today's information landscape weaponizes attention through clickbait headlines, artificial outrage, and algorithmic amplification of divisive content. News cycles that once lasted days now change hourly, creating a constant sense of crisis that exhausts our capacity for thoughtful response. Christians face the challenge of staying informed without being overwhelmed, engaged without being manipulated by information systems designed to maximize profit rather than understanding.

WARRIOR REFLECTION

- **Understanding Truth:** How does biblical discernment differ from both naive acceptance and cynical rejection of information?

Day 11
Finding Truth in a World of Noise

- **Heart Application:** How does the news you consume affect your peace and your view of the world?

MEDITATION SCRIPTURE

"Your word is a lamp to guide my feet and a light for my path." —Psalm 119:105

PRAYER

Heavenly Father, in a world of competing narratives, anchor me in Your unchanging Word. Lord Jesus, You are the way, the truth, and the life. Help me measure all claims against Your perfect standard. Holy Spirit, give me discernment to recognize distortion and clarity to see what's real. Where news creates anxiety, replace it with Your peace that passes understanding. Guide me to information sources that illuminate rather than manipulate. Amen.

BATTLE STRATEGY

FIRST STEP

When you encounter a troubling news story today, practice the "pause and pray" approach: Pause to pray for wisdom, check multiple sources, and consider what Scripture says before responding.

Going Deeper

Create a "truth-seeking" routine: Select one news story this week and research it from multiple perspectives, including those you might disagree with. Note how different sources frame the same events.

Warrior Challenge

Form a "current events discernment group" that meets monthly to discuss major news stories through a biblical lens, praying for those affected and discerning how Christians might respond with truth and grace.

NOTES:

Day 12
Master, Not Mastered

Technology That Serves
Voice of the Heart Reference: Chapter 12: Technology & Data

"You say, 'I am allowed to do anything'—but not everything is good for you. You say, 'I am allowed to do anything'—but not everything is beneficial."
—1 Corinthians 10:23

Today's Theme

Paul's declaration about not being "mastered by anything" speaks with remarkable relevance to our relationship with technology. Though writing centuries before smartphones and social media, he understood a timeless principle: Christians should use tools rather than be used by them. Our devices should serve God's purposes in our lives, not become our masters.

Battlefield Wisdom

Technology has transformed from tools we occasionally used to an environment we constantly inhabit. What began as helpful devices have become extensions of ourselves, changing how we think, relate, and live. This shift matches exactly what Paul warned about—good things becoming masters rather than servants in our lives.

Jesus taught in Matthew 6:22-23: "Your eye is like a lamp that provides light for your body. When your eye is healthy, your whole body is filled with light." What we fix our eyes on—what we give our attention to—fills us either with light or darkness. Our technologies are designed to capture and hold our attention, often directing it toward what profits others rather than what benefits our souls. The solution isn't rejecting technology entirely, but establishing boundaries that ensure it remains our servant rather than our master.

FRONTLINE FOCUS

Today's digital technologies are increasingly designed using the same principles as addictive substances—variable rewards, social validation, and fear of missing out combine to create powerful psychological dependencies. The average person checks their phone 96 times daily—once every 10 minutes of waking life. This constant connectivity often displaces prayer, reflection, and real-world relationships that God designed for our flourishing.

WARRIOR REFLECTION

- **Understanding Truth:** What biblical principles should guide our use of technology?
- **Heart Application:** What technology in your life has shifted from being your tool to becoming your master?

Day 12
Master, Not Mastered

MEDITATION SCRIPTURE

"You say, 'I am allowed to do anything'—but not everything is good for you. And even though 'I am allowed to do anything,' I must not become a slave to anything." —1 Corinthians 6:12

PRAYER

Heavenly Father, You created all good things to be received with thanksgiving and used for Your glory. Lord Jesus, You call me to undivided devotion, loving You with my whole heart, mind, soul, and strength. Holy Spirit, help me use technology as a tool for Your purposes rather than being mastered by it. Show me where digital devices have replaced relationship with You or others. Give me wisdom to establish healthy boundaries. Amen.

BATTLE STRATEGY

FIRST STEP

Create one tech-free zone or time period in your life today. This might be making meals phone-free, not checking devices for the first hour after waking, or designating a room as device-free.

GOING DEEPER

Conduct a week-long "technology audit": Install a screen time tracker on your devices and record how you use them. At week's end, prayerfully evaluate what adjustments would bring your technology use into better alignment with your spiritual priorities.

WARRIOR CHALLENGE

Implement a monthly "digital sabbath"—a 24-hour period completely free from screens and digital devices. Use this time for prayer, nature, face-to-face relationships, and activities that refresh your connection with God and others.

NOTES:

Day 13
Breaking Free from Worldly Systems

Finding God's Economy
Voice of the Heart Reference: Chapter 13: Economic & Social Systems

"And what do you benefit if you gain the whole world but lose your own soul?" —Matthew 16:26

Today's Theme

Jesus's instruction to "seek first his kingdom" offers a radical alternative to the world's priorities. While earthly systems focus on accumulation and status, God's kingdom operates by different principles. Jesus invites us to step into an alternative economy where generosity replaces greed, service replaces status, and relationship replaces transaction.

Battlefield Wisdom

The systems of this world often function like a bonsai tree—they appear to offer growth while actually constraining it. Economic and social structures prune our development to fit predetermined patterns, limiting what we can become. Many Christians feel tension between the world's expectations and God's calling.

Jesus addressed this directly, warning in Matthew 6:24, "No one can serve two masters... You cannot serve God and be enslaved to money." The early church demonstrated a counter-cultural approach. As Acts 2:45 records, "They sold their property and possessions and shared the money with those in need." This wasn't just charity—it was a completely different way of relating to resources. Like branches turning toward sunlight, we're called to orient our lives toward God's kingdom values rather than worldly success.

FRONTLINE FOCUS

Today's consumer capitalism has evolved beyond selling products to selling identities, promising fulfillment through acquisition and status. Social media platforms monetize our attention and relationships, transforming human connection into economic transactions. Career paths increasingly demand total allegiance, making "success" require sacrifice of family, community, and spiritual development. Against these powerful currents, choosing God's economy becomes a radical act of faith and resistance.

WARRIOR REFLECTION

- **Understanding Truth:** How do Jesus's teachings about money and possessions differ from our culture's messages?
- **Heart Application:** In what ways have worldly economic or social systems constrained your spiritual growth or service to God?

Day 13
Breaking Free from Worldly Systems

MEDITATION SCRIPTURE

"Seek the Kingdom of God above all else, and live righteously, and he will give you everything you need." —Matthew 6:33

PRAYER

Heavenly Father, You own the cattle on a thousand hills and provide abundantly for Your children. Lord Jesus, You modeled contentment and generosity, finding Your value not in possessions but in relationship with the Father. Holy Spirit, help me see where I've accepted the world's definitions of success rather than Yours. Give me courage to choose kingdom values even when they contradict cultural expectations. Show me how to use resources for eternal purposes. Amen.

BATTLE STRATEGY

FIRST STEP

Identify one way your resources (time, money, talents) are currently serving worldly values rather than kingdom purposes. Make one specific change today that better aligns this resource with God's priorities.

GOING DEEPER

Create a "kingdom economics" inventory of your major resources (income, possessions, skills, time). For each one, prayerfully consider: "Is this primarily building my kingdom or God's kingdom?" Develop a plan to shift one resource more fully toward kingdom purposes.

WARRIOR CHALLENGE

Form a small group committed to exploring and practicing biblical economics together. Study Scripture's teachings on money and possessions, hold each other accountable for generous living, and find ways to share resources that demonstrate kingdom values to your community.

NOTES:

Day 14
True Wealth in God's Economy

Breaking the Money Trap
Voice of the Heart Reference: Chapter 14: Finance & Economics

"Don't love money; be satisfied with what you have. For God has said, 'I will never fail you. I will never abandon you.'" —Hebrews 13:5

Today's Theme

Jesus's teaching about treasures reveals a profound truth: what we value shapes who we become. He isn't merely giving financial advice but addressing the orientation of our hearts. The things we treasure—what we invest in, save for, and spend on—reveal and reinforce our deepest values.

Battlefield Wisdom

Financial systems often operate through extraction rather than exchange, taking value without giving equivalent return. These systems create dependency through debt, consumption patterns, and artificial scarcity. They whisper that we never have enough and should measure success by material accumulation.

God's economy operates by different principles. Jesus taught: "Give, and you will receive. Your gift will return to you in full—pressed down, shaken together to make room for more, running over, and poured into your lap. The amount you give will determine the amount you get back" (Luke 6:38), inverting the world's focus on getting more.

Scripture emphasizes generosity, with 2 Corinthians 9:6 reminding us: "Remember this—a farmer who plants only a few seeds will get a small crop. But the one who plants generously will get a generous crop." Following these principles transforms our relationship with possessions.

FRONTLINE FOCUS

In an age of targeted advertising, one-click purchasing, and buy-now-pay-later financing, financial discipline requires intentionality. Digital payments remove the psychological friction of spending, while social media highlights what others have that we don't. These technologies combine with our tendency toward discontentment to create conditions for financial bondage unless we cultivate contentment and wisdom.

WARRIOR REFLECTION

- **Understanding Truth:** How does Scripture's teaching about money differ from common financial advice?

- **Heart Application:** In what area of your financial life do you most need to apply God's principles rather than the world's?

Day 14
True Wealth in God's Economy

MEDITATION SCRIPTURE

> "Don't store up treasures here on earth, where moths eat them and rust destroys them, and where thieves break in and steal. Store your treasures in heaven... Wherever your treasure is, there the desires of your heart will also be."
> —Matthew 6:19-21

PRAYER

Heavenly Father, all I have comes from You. Help me steward it faithfully. Lord Jesus, realign my heart to treasure what truly matters. Holy Spirit, free me from materialism and fill me with generosity that reflects God's character. Amen.

BATTLE STRATEGY

FIRST STEP

Take a "financial sabbath" today by avoiding all unnecessary spending. Use this practice to reflect on what drives your purchasing decisions.

GOING DEEPER

Track every expenditure for one week, then prayerfully review the list. For each purchase, ask: "Did this align with God's values? Did it build treasure on earth or in heaven?" Identify one spending pattern to change based on your findings.

WARRIOR CHALLENGE

Commit to a "generosity experiment" for three months: Increase your giving by a specific percentage, reduce debt by a specific amount, or simplify your lifestyle in a significant way. Document how this shift affects your relationship with God and others.

NOTES:

Day 15
Citizenship in Two Kingdoms

Living Under God's Authority
Voice of the Heart Reference: Chapter 15: Government

"Give to Caesar what belongs to Caesar, and give to God what belongs to God."
—Matthew 22:21

Today's Theme

Paul's teaching on government reminds us of the tension Christians live in—we're citizens of earthly nations while ultimately belonging to God's kingdom. This dual citizenship creates both responsibilities and challenges as we navigate political systems while maintaining our primary allegiance to Christ.

Battlefield Wisdom

Government systems can both help and hinder human flourishing. At their best, they maintain order, protect the vulnerable, and promote justice. At their worst, they can become tools of oppression, division, and control. Christians are called to engage thoughtfully with these systems, neither blindly accepting nor completely rejecting them.

Jesus demonstrated this balanced approach when asked about paying taxes, saying, "Give to Caesar what belongs to Caesar, and give to God what belongs to God" (Matthew 22:21). He acknowledged legitimate governmental authority while reminding us of our higher allegiance. Similarly, when human authority conflicts with divine commands, we follow the example of the apostles who declared, "We must obey God rather than any human authority" (Acts 5:29). As Paul reminds us, "We are citizens of heaven, where the Lord Jesus Christ lives" (Philippians 3:20), and this shapes how we engage with earthly political systems. Rather than being defined by partisan identities, we're called to be defined by Christ our King.

FRONTLINE FOCUS

In today's politically polarized culture, many Christians find their primary identity in political affiliation rather than in Christ. Social media algorithms and partisan news sources reinforce tribal thinking, making political opponents seem not just wrong but evil. This environment makes living as citizens of God's kingdom increasingly counter-cultural, requiring us to evaluate political positions through Scripture rather than evaluating Scripture through political lenses.

WARRIOR REFLECTION

- **Understanding Truth:** What principles does Scripture provide for relating to government authorities?

Day 15
Citizenship in Two Kingdoms

- **Heart Application:** How has your political identity influenced your Christian identity, and vice versa?

MEDITATION SCRIPTURE

"Everyone must submit to governing authorities. For all authority comes from God, and those in positions of authority have been placed there by God." —Romans 13:1

PRAYER

Heavenly Father, You establish authorities for the good of society, yet remain the ultimate Sovereign over all. Lord Jesus, You submitted to earthly authorities even while declaring a kingdom not of this world. Holy Spirit, give me wisdom to navigate political systems without being defined by them. Help me honor governing authorities while maintaining my primary allegiance to God. Guard my heart against partisan division that might damage my witness for the kingdom. Amen.

BATTLE STRATEGY

FIRST STEP

Choose one issue facing your community where you could take practical action beyond political debate. Find a tangible way to serve others around this issue that demonstrates Christ's love in action.

Going Deeper

Examine your political news consumption. For one week, read perspectives from sources you don't typically agree with, asking God to help you understand different viewpoints through a biblical lens rather than a partisan one.

Warrior Challenge

Start a "kingdom politics" discussion group committed to studying what Scripture teaches about government, justice, and citizenship. Develop guidelines ensuring respectful dialogue across political differences, focusing on biblical principles rather than partisan positions.

NOTES:

Day 16
Building Bridges of Unity

Breaking Down Walls
Voice of the Heart Reference: Chapter 16: Social Structures

"There is no longer Jew or Gentile, slave or free, male and female. For you are all one in Christ Jesus." —Galatians 3:28

Today's Theme

Paul's declaration that our differences disappear "in Christ Jesus" wasn't just theological theory—it was a revolutionary statement in a rigidly divided world. While society builds walls between people based on countless distinctions, Christ tears these walls down, creating a new community where our primary identity is found in Him, not in social categories.

Battlefield Wisdom

Social structures powerfully shape how we see ourselves and others. They create rules about who belongs where, who deserves respect, and how people should interact across differences. These structures often pressure us to conform to expectations rather than express our authentic selves, and they can divide communities that should be united.

Jesus consistently challenged these divisive structures. He touched those considered untouchable, ate with those labeled unworthy, and built relationships across social boundaries. The early church continued this counter-cultural approach, forming communities in which, as Acts 4:32 describes, "All the believers were united in heart and mind" despite their diverse backgrounds. James reinforced this value, warning strongly against favoritism based on social status: "My dear brothers and sisters, how can you claim to have faith in our glorious Lord Jesus Christ if you favor some people over others?" (James 2:1-9). As followers of Christ the Reconciler, we're called to be bridge-builders in a wall-building world.

FRONTLINE FOCUS

In an era of increasing polarization, algorithms, and media channels sort us into ever-narrower identity groups, emphasizing differences over common humanity. Digital spaces often incentivize conflict over connection, with outrage driving engagement more effectively than understanding. Against this cultural current, Christians are called to the radical work of reconciliation—creating spaces where human divisions are transcended through our shared identity in Christ.

Day 16
Building Bridges of Unity

WARRIOR REFLECTION

- **Understanding Truth:** How does our identity in Christ transform how we should relate to human categories and divisions?
- **Heart Application:** What social divisions or groupings most strongly influence how you see yourself and others?

MEDITATION SCRIPTURE

"For Christ himself has brought peace to us. He united Jews and Gentiles into one people when, in his own body on the cross, he broke down the wall of hostility that separated us." —Ephesians 2:14

PRAYER

Heavenly Father, You created every person in Your image, giving each one inherent dignity and worth. Lord Jesus, through Your sacrifice You broke down the dividing walls of hostility, creating one new humanity out of previously divided groups. Holy Spirit, forgive me for the times I've accepted worldly divisions rather than embracing the unity You created. Help me see beyond labels to recognize the image of God in every person. Give me courage to build bridges where others build walls. Amen.

Battle Strategy

First Step

Intentionally connect today with someone you might not normally interact with due to social divisions (different generation, cultural background, political view, etc.). Approach with genuine curiosity and respect.

Going Deeper

Examine your friendship circle, media consumption, and daily interactions. Where do you see homogeneity that might limit your understanding of others? Choose one concrete way to expand your perspective by crossing a social boundary this week.

Warrior Challenge

Host a "bridging differences" dinner or event that intentionally brings together people from different backgrounds around a shared meal or purpose. Create space for authentic sharing of stories and perspectives that builds understanding across social divides.

NOTES:

_____

_____

_____

_____

_____

Day 17
Finding True Security
Where Our Protection Comes From
Voice of the Heart Reference: Chapter 17: Security & Welfare Systems

> *"Some nations boast of their chariots and horses,
> but we boast in the name of the LORD our God."*
> —Psalm 20:7

Today's Theme

The psalmist offers a timeless reminder about where true security comes from. While human systems promise protection and welfare, God alone offers unfailing refuge. This doesn't mean we ignore human provisions for safety and security, but it does mean we recognize their limitations and place our ultimate trust in the Lord.

Battlefield Wisdom

Security and welfare systems shape what we consider safe, secure, and sufficient. From healthcare to emergency services, from social safety nets to military protection, these systems provide valuable support. However, they can also foster dependency, create false security, and sometimes control rather than serve those they're meant to protect.

Jesus addressed our tendency to trust in earthly security when He taught, "That is why I tell you not to worry about everyday life—whether you have enough food and drink, or enough clothes to wear... Look at the birds. They don't plant or harvest or store food in barns, for your heavenly Father feeds them." (Matthew 6:25-26). This doesn't mean irresponsibility, but a reordered trust—seeking God's kingdom first while making wise use of earthly provisions. When we balance appropriate participation in human systems with ultimate reliance on God our Provider, we experience true security.

FRONTLINE FOCUS

Today's culture markets security products and services that promise to protect us from an ever-expanding list of threats, creating a perpetual anxiety that can only be addressed through more consumption. Digital security threats and surveillance technologies combine to create a climate of fear that tempts us to place our trust in elaborate protection systems rather than in God. Christians are called to a different response—prudent preparation without paranoia, wise stewardship without worry.

WARRIOR REFLECTION

- **Understanding Truth:** How does Scripture balance personal responsibility for security with trust in God's protection?

- **Heart Application:** What security systems (financial, health, protection) do you tend to put your ultimate trust in?

Day 17
Finding True Security

MEDITATION SCRIPTURE

> "It is better to take refuge in the LORD than to trust in people. It is better to take refuge in the LORD than to trust in princes."
> —Psalm 118:8-9

PRAYER

Heavenly Father, You are my fortress and deliverer, my ultimate source of security in an uncertain world. Lord Jesus, You taught us to trust the Father for our needs while using wisdom in our earthly affairs. Holy Spirit, help me discern the line between responsible preparation and faithless worry. When I'm tempted to place my trust in human provisions, remind me that You alone are my unshakable fortress. Give me wisdom to participate in earthly security systems while keeping my ultimate confidence in You. Amen.

BATTLE STRATEGY

FIRST STEP

Identify one area where worry about security (financial, physical, health, etc.) affects your peace. Write down both the practical steps you can take AND a prayer surrendering the outcome to God.

GOING DEEPER

Examine your security practices to identify where fear might be driving decisions rather than wisdom. For one week, when security concerns arise, ask: "Is this a prudent precaution or am I seeking absolute control?"

Warrior Challenge

Create a "trust building" plan addressing an area where security concerns have led to excessive worry. Balance practical preparation with specific trust-building spiritual practices (Scripture memory, prayer, thanksgiving) that transfer your ultimate confidence from systems to God.

NOTES:

DAY 18
WHOLENESS IN BODY AND SPIRIT

HONORING GOD'S TEMPLE
Voice of the Heart Reference: Chapter 18: Health & Wellness

"Don't you realize that your body is the temple of the Holy Spirit, who lives in you and was given to you by God? You do not belong to yourself, for God bought you with a high price. So you must honor God with your body."
—1 Corinthians 6:19-20

TODAY'S THEME

John's prayer reveals God's desire for wholeness in every aspect of our lives—both physical and spiritual. Unlike modern approaches that often separate body and soul, Scripture presents a unified view where physical health and spiritual wellbeing are interconnected parts of God's design for human flourishing.

BATTLEFIELD WISDOM

Health systems shape how we care for our bodies. While modern healthcare offers benefits, it can reduce humans to collections of symptoms rather than whole beings created in God's image, focusing on managing symptoms instead of addressing root causes.

Scripture offers an integrated approach. Paul reminds us in 1 Corinthians 6:19-20: "Your bodies are temples of the Holy Spirit." Jesus demonstrated concern for both physical and spiritual healing, as when He healed the paralyzed man, first saying, "My child, your sins are forgiven," and then, "Stand up, pick up your mat, and go home!" (Mark 2:5, 11). God's approach integrates physical, emotional, and spiritual dimensions as connected aspects of our being.

FRONTLINE FOCUS

Today's wellness culture offers competing approaches—from technological healthcare to Eastern-rooted practices. Social media promotes unrealistic standards and quick-fix solutions, while stress and sedentary lifestyles create health challenges. Christians need discernment to embrace legitimate advances while maintaining a biblical understanding of the body as God's temple.

WARRIOR REFLECTION

- **Understanding Truth:** How does Scripture's integrated view of physical and spiritual health differ from typical modern approaches?

- **Heart Application:** How integrated or separated are your approaches to physical and spiritual health in daily practice?

Day 18
Wholeness in Body and Spirit

MEDITATION SCRIPTURE

"Dear friend, I hope all is well with you and that you are as healthy in body as you are strong in spirit." —3 John 1:2

PRAYER

Heavenly Father, thank You for creating me as a whole person—body, mind, and spirit. You designed each aspect to work in harmony. Lord Jesus, You demonstrated perfect integration of physical and spiritual wellness, healing both body and soul. Holy Spirit, You dwell within me, making my body Your temple. Help me care for my physical health as an act of stewardship, honoring the body where You dwell. Guide me to balance appropriate use of medical resources with trust in Your healing power. Amen.

BATTLE STRATEGY

FIRST STEP

Choose one health practice today that honors both body and spirit, such as taking a prayer walk, preparing a nutritious meal with gratitude, or practicing deep breathing while meditating on Scripture.

GOING DEEPER

Create a "temple care assessment" by evaluating how your sleep, nutrition, movement, and stress management practices affect your spiritual vitality. Choose one area to improve this week, treating it as spiritual stewardship rather than mere self-care.

WARRIOR CHALLENGE

Form a "whole-person wellness" group that supports each other in caring for body, mind, and spirit together. Meet regularly to exercise, pray, study Scripture about health, and hold each other accountable for honoring God with your bodies.

NOTES:

Day 19
Justice That Reflects God's Heart

Beyond Systems to True Fairness
Voice of the Heart Reference: Chapter 19: Law, Order & Justice

> *"Learn to do good. Seek justice. Help the oppressed. Defend the cause of orphans. Fight for the rights of widows."* —Isaiah 1:17

Today's Theme

Micah's powerful question—"what does the LORD require?"—receives an equally powerful answer: justice, mercy, and humility. These three qualities form the foundation of God's approach to justice, balancing righteous standards with compassionate application and a humble recognition of our own need for grace.

Battlefield Wisdom

Justice systems shape what we consider fair and how we respond to wrongs. While these systems are necessary for maintaining order, they can sometimes create injustice through unequal application of laws, complexity that favors those with resources, and approaches that focus on punishment rather than restoration.

Jesus consistently demonstrated God's heart for true justice. When confronted with the woman caught in adultery, He upheld the law while challenging its selective application (John 8:1-11). Throughout Scripture, God shows special concern for those most vulnerable to injustice. Isaiah 1:17 urges us to "Learn to do good. Seek justice. Help the oppressed..." Psalm 146:7-9 celebrates how God "gives justice to the oppressed and food to the hungry. The LORD frees the prisoners. The LORD opens the eyes of the blind. The LORD lifts up those who are weighed down. The LORD loves the godly. The LORD protects the foreigners among us. He cares for the orphans and widows."

FRONTLINE FOCUS

In today's complex society, justice issues are often reduced to partisan political positions rather than biblical imperatives. Social media amplifies outrage while rarely promoting understanding of complex systems. Christians face the challenge of pursuing true biblical justice that transcends political categorization—defending the vulnerable, promoting fair systems, and balancing accountability with restoration in a way that reflects God's heart rather than cultural agendas.

WARRIOR REFLECTION

- **Understanding Truth:** How do justice, mercy, and humility work together in God's approach to wrongs?

Day 19
Justice That Reflects God's Heart

- **Heart Application:** Where have you seen justice systems succeed or fail in your experience, and how might biblical principles transform these systems?

MEDITATION SCRIPTURE

"No, O people, the LORD has told you what is good, and this is what he requires of you: to do what is right, to love mercy, and to walk humbly with your God." —Micah 6:8

PRAYER

Heavenly Father, Your justice is perfect, balancing accountability with restoration, never separating truth from love. Lord Jesus, You satisfied both justice and mercy through Your sacrifice, making forgiveness possible without compromising righteousness. Holy Spirit, align my heart with God's when it comes to fairness and mercy. Help me recognize injustice and give me courage to speak up for those without voice. Keep me from harsh judgment while maintaining clear standards of right and wrong. Amen.

BATTLE STRATEGY

FIRST STEP

Research one justice issue in your community (homelessness, food insecurity, access to education, etc.). Find an organization addressing this issue and take one specific action to support their work.

Going Deeper

Study a justice passage in Scripture (such as Isaiah 58, Amos 5, or Luke 4:16-21) and journal about how it challenges or confirms your current understanding of biblical justice. Identify one way to align your perspective more fully with God's heart.

Warrior Challenge

Commit to ongoing engagement with a specific justice issue that God places on your heart. Develop a three-part approach including: (1) direct service to affected individuals, (2) learning about systemic factors, and (3) advocating for changes that promote biblical justice.

NOTES:

Day 20
The Path of Peace

From Conflict to Connection
Voice of the Heart Reference:
Chapter 20: The Military Industrial Complex

"Do all that you can to live in peace with everyone." —Romans 12:18

Today's Theme

Jesus's blessing on peacemakers reveals God's heart for reconciliation rather than conflict. By calling peacemakers "children of God," Jesus indicates that creating peace reflects the very character of our heavenly Father. In a world that often glorifies power and force, Christ calls His followers to a different path—one that builds bridges rather than barriers.

Battlefield Wisdom

Military and security systems shape how we respond to threats and conflicts. While protection from genuine dangers is necessary, these systems can sometimes perpetuate fear, division, and ongoing conflict rather than working toward lasting peace.

Scripture presents an alternative vision. Isaiah prophesied: "The LORD will mediate between nations and will settle international disputes. They will hammer their swords into plowshares and their spears into pruning hooks" (Isaiah 2:4), transforming instruments of destruction into tools for cultivation and growth. Jesus taught His followers to "love your enemies! Pray for those who persecute you!" (Matthew 5:44), challenging the natural human response to threats. And Paul instructed, "Do all that you can to live in peace with everyone." (Romans 12:18). These teachings don't ignore real dangers but offer a different approach to addressing them—one based on transforming relationships rather than simply overpowering opponents.

FRONTLINE FOCUS

In our polarized society, conflict resolution skills have been replaced by conflict escalation tactics. Social media platforms reward outrage and "dunking" on opponents rather than understanding and reconciliation. Personal conflicts quickly become public spectacles through digital sharing. Against this backdrop, Christians who practice the challenging art of peacemaking—truly seeking to understand others, finding common ground, and pursuing reconciliation—stand out as countercultural representatives of Christ's kingdom.

WARRIOR REFLECTION

- **Understanding Truth:** How does Jesus's approach to conflict and enemies differ from natural human responses?
- **Heart Application:** How do you typically respond to conflict in your personal relationships?

Day 20
The Path of Peace

MEDITATION SCRIPTURE

"God blesses those who work for peace, for they will be called the children of God." —Matthew 5:9

PRAYER

Heavenly Father, in You we find the perfect balance of justice and peace, never compromising one for the other. Lord Jesus, You are the Prince of Peace who taught us to love enemies, pray for persecutors, and seek reconciliation. Holy Spirit, transform me into a true peacemaker who reflects God's character. Where I'm tempted to respond with force or anger, teach me Your way of reconciliation. Help me build bridges where others create walls and pursue peace without compromising truth. Amen.

BATTLE STRATEGY

FIRST STEP

Identify one relationship or situation where conflict exists in your life. Take one specific step toward peace today—whether initiating a difficult conversation, offering forgiveness, or seeking to understand the other perspective.

GOING DEEPER

Practice the "perspective pause" this week when conflicts arise. Before responding, pause to consider: "What might this look like from the other person's perspective?

What underlying needs or fears might be driving their behavior?" Allow this reflection to shape your response.

Warrior Challenge

Develop your conflict transformation skills by studying biblical peacemaking principles. Find a resource on Christian conflict resolution, apply its insights to a current relationship challenge, and share what you're learning with someone else struggling with conflict.

NOTES:

DAY 21
RECOGNIZING THE ENEMY'S ARSENAL

UNDERSTANDING THE BATTLE PLAN
Voice of the Heart Reference: Chapter 21: The Enemy's Weaponry

"Put on all of God's armor so that you will be able to stand firm against all strategies of the devil."
—Ephesians 6:11

TODAY'S THEME

Paul's statement that we shouldn't be "unaware of his schemes" highlights an important truth: understanding the enemy's tactics gives us a strategic advantage. Just as military leaders study their opponents' strategies, Christians benefit from recognizing the specific ways spiritual attacks target our hearts and minds.

BATTLEFIELD WISDOM

The enemy doesn't just attack randomly—he employs specific weapons designed to undermine our faith and fruitfulness. These coordinated attacks target three vital areas: our purpose (who God made us to be), our peace (our connection to truth), and our passion (our love-fueled energy for God's kingdom).

Jesus faced these same attacks during His temptation in the wilderness (Matthew 4:1-11). The devil targeted His identity ("If you are the Son of God..."), tried to distort truth with out-of-context Scripture, and attempted to redirect His passion toward worldly power rather than God's purpose. Jesus countered each attack with God's Word, showing us how to stand firm when similar weapons are used against us. As Paul reminds us in Ephesians 6:11-12, "Put on all of God's armor so that you will be able to stand firm against all strategies of the devil. For we are not fighting against flesh-and-blood enemies, but against evil rulers and authorities of the unseen world." By recognizing these schemes, we can respond with the spiritual weapons God provides rather than being caught off guard.

FRONTLINE FOCUS

Today's spiritual warfare often happens through digital means—negative thought patterns reinforced by social media comparison, doubts cultivated through skeptical content, and distractions engineered to fragment our attention and diminish our effectiveness. The enemy has adapted ancient tactics to modern technology, making awareness of these strategies essential for anyone seeking to maintain spiritual vitality in a digital age.

WARRIOR REFLECTION

- **Understanding Truth:** What does Scripture reveal about Satan's specific tactics and strategies?

Day 21
Recognizing the Enemy's Arsenal

- **Heart Application:** Which area—purpose, peace, or passion—seems most under attack in your life right now?

MEDITATION SCRIPTURE

"so that Satan will not outsmart us. For we are familiar with his evil schemes."
—2 Corinthians 2:11

PRAYER

Heavenly Father, thank You for exposing the enemy's tactics through Your Word so I can stand firm against them. Lord Jesus, You perfectly countered every temptation and attack, showing us how to respond with truth. Holy Spirit, give me discernment to recognize when my purpose, peace, or passion is under attack. Help me see the source of discouragements, doubts, and distractions in my life. I submit to God and resist the enemy's schemes, trusting in Christ's victory. Amen.

BATTLE STRATEGY

FIRST STEP

Make an "attack recognition" list today, identifying three specific ways the enemy typically targets you. Next to each, write a specific Scripture that counters this attack.

Going Deeper

Create a "spiritual armor check" to use daily this week. Each morning, review Ephesians 6:10-18 and assess which piece of armor you most need that day based on the attacks you're experiencing. Intentionally "put on" this protection through prayer and meditation on relevant Scripture.

Warrior Challenge

Form a spiritual warfare prayer group that meets regularly to learn about enemy tactics, share areas of vulnerability, and pray for one another's protection and victory. Develop strategies for spiritual support during intense seasons of attack.

NOTES:

DAY 22
DEFENDING YOUR TRUE IDENTITY

STANDING FIRM IN WHO GOD MADE YOU
Voice of the Heart Reference: Chapter 22: Weapons Against Purpose

> *"But you are not like that, for you are a chosen people. You are royal priests, a holy nation, God's very own possession. As a result, you can show others the goodness of God, for he called you out of the darkness into his wonderful light."*
> —1 Peter 2:9

TODAY'S THEME

"You made all the delicate, inner parts of my body and knit me together in my mother's womb." (Psalm 139). David's declaration is a beautiful truth that too often stands in stark contrast to the identity attacks we often face. God has crafted each of us with purpose and intentionality, creating us for specific good works that express His character in the world.

BATTLEFIELD WISDOM

The enemy targets our identity through weapons that disconnect us from who God made us. These attacks include neglect (making us feel invisible), conformity (pressuring us to fit improper molds), comparison (measuring against others not God's calling), and ignorance (limiting awareness of possibilities).

Scripture reinforces our identity against these attacks. When neglect makes us feel invisible, Psalm 139 reminds us God knit us with purpose. When conformity pressures us, Romans 12:2 warns, "Don't copy the behavior and customs of this world, but let God transform you into a new person by changing the way you think." When comparison tempts us, 2 Corinthians 10:12 warns: "Oh, don't worry; we wouldn't dare say that we are as wonderful as these other men who tell you how important they are! But they are only comparing themselves with each other, using themselves as the standard of measurement. How ignorant!"

When ignorance limits us, Jeremiah 33:3 invites us: "Ask me and I will tell you remarkable secrets you do not know about things to come." Our identity is secured in God's design.

FRONTLINE FOCUS

Today, we're offered manufactured self-concepts through brands, careers, politics, and digital personas. Social media encourages curated identities over authenticity, while advertising suggests worth comes from consumption. Against these forces, anchoring in God's definition of who we are becomes spiritual resistance.

Day 22
Defending Your True Identity

Warrior Reflection

- **Understanding Truth:** How does God's perspective on our identity differ from the world's measures of worth and importance?
- **Heart Application:** Which weapon against your purpose—neglect, conformity, comparison, or ignorance—has most effectively disconnected you from your God-given identity?

Meditation Scripture

"For we are God's masterpiece. He has created us anew in Christ Jesus, so we can do the good things he planned for us long ago."
—Ephesians 2:10

Prayer

Heavenly Father, thank You for creating me as Your masterpiece with unique purpose. When neglect makes me feel invisible, remind me that You see me completely. Lord Jesus, You lived with perfect authenticity, never swayed by others' expectations or demands. Holy Spirit, when conformity pressures me to fit in, help me remember You made me to reflect a unique aspect of God's nature. When comparison steals my joy, redirect my focus to the unique calling You've given me. I claim my identity as Your beloved child. Amen.

Battle Strategy

First Step

Take 15 minutes today to list five specific ways God has uniquely designed you (gifts, experiences, passions, etc.). For each one, write how this aspect of your identity might be used for His purposes.

Going Deeper

Create an "identity shield" by selecting five Scripture verses that declare who you are in Christ. Write these on a card and read them aloud daily for a week, especially when facing attacks on your purpose and identity.

Warrior Challenge

Develop an "identity mentoring" relationship—either receive guidance from someone who can help you discover and embrace your God-given design, or help someone else recognize and step into their unique purpose in God's kingdom.

NOTES:

_____

_____

_____

_____

_____

_____

Day 23
Standing Firm in God's Truth

Finding Peace Amid Deception
Voice of the Heart Reference: Chapter 23: Weapons Against Peace

> *"You will keep in perfect peace all who trust in you, all whose thoughts are fixed on you!"*
> —Isaiah 26:3

Today's Theme

Jesus connects truth directly with freedom, showing that living in reality—as God defines it—liberates us from deception's bondage. When we build our lives on God's unchanging truth rather than shifting opinions or manipulated information, we find a peace that remains steady even when everything around us seems uncertain.

Battlefield Wisdom

The enemy specifically targets our peace through weapons designed to disconnect us from truth. These attacks include lies and deception (replacing reality with falsehood), noise and confusion (overwhelming us with information that clouds clear thinking), insufficiency (creating artificial scarcity amid God's abundance), and division (separating us from others who might help us see truth).

God provides powerful defenses against these attacks throughout Scripture. When lies threaten our peace, Psalm 119:160 reminds us: "The very essence of your words is truth; all your just regulations will stand forever." When noise overwhelms us, Jesus's example of withdrawing to the wilderness to pray (Luke 5:16) shows us how to find clarity. When insufficiency creates anxiety, Philippians 4:19 assures us: "This same God who takes care of me will supply all your needs from his glorious riches, which have been given to us in Christ Jesus." And when division isolates us, Ephesians 2:14 declares: "For Christ himself has brought peace to us. He united Jews and Gentiles into one people when, in his own body on the cross, he broke down the wall of hostility that separated us."

FRONTLINE FOCUS

Today's information ecosystem is explicitly designed to capture and manipulate attention through emotional triggering, tribal signaling, and algorithmic amplification of extreme content. Deepfake technology, AI-generated text, and sophisticated propaganda make distinguishing truth from fiction increasingly difficult. In this environment, developing biblical discernment becomes not just spiritually important but practically essential for maintaining mental and emotional wellbeing.

Day 23
Standing Firm in God's Truth

WARRIOR REFLECTION

- **Understanding Truth:** What practices does Scripture recommend for discerning truth from falsehood?
- **Heart Application:** Which weapon against your peace—lies, noise, insufficiency, or division—most effectively disrupts your connection to God's truth?

MEDITATION SCRIPTURE

> *"I have told you all this so that you may have peace in me. Here on earth you will have many trials and sorrows. But take heart, because I have overcome the world."*
> —John 16:33

PRAYER

Heavenly Father, You are the source of all truth in a universe where deception abounds. Lord Jesus, You declared Yourself to be "the way, the truth, and the life," offering the ultimate reality check for every falsehood. Holy Spirit, You are the Spirit of truth who guides us into all truth. Anchor me firmly in Your reality when deception surrounds me. When lies tempt me to believe what contradicts Your Word, sharpen my discernment. When noise and information overwhelm me, guide me to stillness where I can hear Your voice. Amen.

BATTLE STRATEGY

FIRST STEP

Practice a "truth filter" today when consuming information: For one significant piece of news or social media content, ask: "What's the evidence?", "Who benefits if I believe this?", and "How does this align with Scripture?"

GOING DEEPER

Implement a daily "peace practice" combining truth and stillness: Spend 10 minutes reading Scripture followed by 5 minutes of silent reflection, asking God to reveal any lies you've believed and replace them with His truth.

WARRIOR CHALLENGE

Create a "truth circle" with trusted believers committed to helping each other discern truth from deception. Establish regular communication where you can discuss challenging issues, check perspectives against Scripture, and pray for each other's peace and clarity.

NOTES:

_____

_____

_____

_____

_____

Day 24
Keeping Your Spiritual Fire Burning

Protecting Your Passion
Voice of the Heart Reference: Chapter 24: Weapons Against Passion

"Never be lazy, but work hard and serve the Lord enthusiastically." —Romans 12:11

Today's Theme

Paul's encouragement to "keep your spiritual fervor" acknowledges an important truth: the fire of passion for God and His purposes requires intentional tending. Like a physical flame that needs fuel, oxygen, and protection from extinguishers, our spiritual passion needs regular attention to remain vibrant and effective.

Battlefield Wisdom

The enemy targets our passion through weapons that diminish spiritual energy. These include doubt (undermining confidence), exhaustion (depleting resources), greed (redirecting desires toward material gain), and disappointment (using setbacks to justify giving up).

Scripture provides antidotes to these passion-killers. For doubt, Hebrews 11:1 reminds us: "Faith shows the reality of what we hope for; it is the evidence of things we cannot see." For exhaustion, Jesus offers this invitation in Matthew 11:28: "Come to me, all of you who are weary and carry heavy burdens, and I will give you rest." For greed, 1 Timothy 6:6 declares: "Yet true godliness with contentment is itself great wealth." For disappointment, Galatians 6:9 encourages us to "not get tired of doing what is good. At just the right time we will reap a harvest of blessing if we don't give up." The Holy Spirit remains our ultimate source of passion.

FRONTLINE FOCUS

In our achievement-oriented, productivity-obsessed culture, burnout has become epidemic. Digital technologies that promise convenience often create constant accessibility, blurring boundaries between work and rest. Social media's highlight reels foster comparison that dampens motivation. These cultural forces combine with spiritual attack to create perfect conditions for passion depletion unless we intentionally cultivate practices that sustain spiritual energy and motivation.

WARRIOR REFLECTION

- **Understanding Truth:** How does Scripture describe the relationship between passion, purpose, and perseverance in the Christian life?

- **Heart Application:** Which weapon against your passion—doubt, exhaustion, greed, or disappointment—most effectively drains your spiritual energy?

Day 24
Keeping Your Spiritual Fire Burning

MEDITATION SCRIPTURE

"But those who trust in the LORD will find new strength. They will soar high on wings like eagles. They will run and not grow weary. They will walk and not faint." —Isaiah 40:31

PRAYER

Heavenly Father, You are the eternal flame whose passion never diminishes or wanes. Lord Jesus, You demonstrated passionate commitment to the Father's will, persevering even through suffering. Holy Spirit, You are the fire within me, igniting my heart with love for God and others. Rekindle the flame of passion in my heart when it grows dim. When doubt makes me hesitate, strengthen my faith. When exhaustion depletes me, lead me to Your restoring presence. Fill me with the fire of Your presence. Amen.

BATTLE STRATEGY

FIRST STEP

Identify your current "passion level" for God and His purposes on a scale of 1-10. Then choose one specific passion-building activity today that historically has rekindled your spiritual fire.

GOING DEEPER

Create a "passion protection plan" by identifying your top three passion-drainers and developing specific strategies to counter each one. Include both spiritual practices (prayer, worship, Scripture) and practical adjustments (rest, boundaries, community).

Warrior Challenge

Establish a "passion partnership" with another believer where you meet monthly to share what's igniting or diminishing your spiritual passion. Hold each other accountable for maintaining passion-building practices and celebrate evidence of renewed spiritual fervor in each other's lives.

NOTES:

_____

_____

_____

_____

_____

_____

_____

_____

_____

Day 25
Awakening to Spiritual Warfare

A Call to Stand Firm
Voice of the Heart Reference: Chapter 25: A Call to Arms

"We are human, but we don't wage war as humans do. We use God's mighty weapons, not worldly weapons, to knock down the strongholds of human reasoning and to destroy false arguments." —2 Corinthians 10:3-4

Today's Theme

Paul's battle cry reminds us that spiritual warfare isn't optional for Christians—it's an inevitable reality of following Christ in a fallen world. His instruction to "be strong in the Lord" reveals an important truth: our strength for this battle comes not from our own resources but from God's mighty power working through us.

Battlefield Wisdom

Recognizing the spiritual battle is the first step toward victory. When we understand our struggles have spiritual dimensions, we gain clarity about effective responses. These attacks on purpose, peace, and passion are coordinated strategies to diminish our kingdom effectiveness.

God equips us for this battle. Ephesians 6:13-18 details our spiritual armor—truth, righteousness, gospel readiness, faith, salvation, God's Word, and prayer. As 1 John 4:4 assures, "But you belong to God, my dear children. You have already won a victory over those people, because the Spirit who lives in you is greater than the spirit who lives in the world." Our confidence comes from Christ's victory: "In this world you will have trouble. But take heart! I have overcome the world" (John 16:33).

FRONTLINE FOCUS

Contemporary culture often either completely dismisses spiritual warfare (reducing everything to psychological or sociological explanations) or sensationalizes it (focusing on dramatic manifestations while missing everyday battles). Many Christians have been functionally disarmed by adopting materialistic worldviews that leave no room for spiritual realities. Reclaiming biblical understanding of spiritual warfare provides essential perspective for navigating challenges in a world where unseen forces actively oppose God's purposes.

WARRIOR REFLECTION

- **Understanding Truth:** How does Scripture describe the reality and nature of spiritual warfare?
- **Heart Application:** Which aspects of spiritual warfare have you tended to overlook or underestimate in your life?

Day 25
Awakening to Spiritual Warfare

MEDITATION SCRIPTURE

"A final word: Be strong in the Lord and in his mighty power. Put on all of God's armor so that you will be able to stand firm against all strategies of the devil." —Ephesians 6:10-11

PRAYER

Heavenly Father, You are the Lord of hosts, the commander of heaven's armies who fights on behalf of Your people. Lord Jesus, through Your death and resurrection You have already secured the ultimate victory over every dark force. Holy Spirit, awaken me to the spiritual dimensions of the challenges I face. Where I've been blind to the enemy's schemes, give me discernment to recognize his tactics. Help me stand firm in Your truth when lies surround me, and to wield the sword of Your Word against deception. Amen.

BATTLE STRATEGY

FIRST STEP

Take inventory of your spiritual armor today. For each piece mentioned in Ephesians 6:13-18, rate how effectively you're utilizing it (1-10), and identify one specific way you could strengthen your weakest area.

GOING DEEPER

Create a "spiritual battleground map" identifying the three areas where you most frequently experience spiritual attack. For each one, develop a specific battle plan including: Scripture to memorize, prayers to pray, and godly counsel to seek.

WARRIOR CHALLENGE

Establish a regular "spiritual perimeter check" with a trusted prayer partner where you review areas of vulnerability, share insights about enemy tactics, and pray for each other's protection and victory. Meet weekly for at least a month to develop this spiritual discipline.

NOTES:

DAY 26
FINDING YOUR GOD-GIVEN PATH

THE JOURNEY TO AUTHENTIC LIVING
Voice of the Heart Reference:
Chapter 26: The Road to Purpose, Peace, and Passion

"Trust in the LORD with all your heart; do not depend on your own understanding. Seek his will in all you do, and he will show you which path to take." —Proverbs 3:5-6

TODAY'S THEME

David's confident declaration reveals that God doesn't hide His path from us—He actively "makes it known." This divine guidance isn't just about avoiding wrong turns but about discovering the fullness of life God intends. The path leads not just to right behavior but to joy and pleasure in God's presence.

BATTLEFIELD WISDOM

Finding God's path requires putting knowledge into action. James 1:22 warns us: "But don't just listen to God's word. You must do what it says. Otherwise, you are only fooling yourselves." Transformation happens when we actively live out what God wants through His Spirit.

This path integrates our purpose (who God made us), peace (alignment with truth), and passion (energy for His kingdom). Together, these create a resilient foundation, like what Ecclesiastes 4:12 describes: "A person standing alone can be attacked and defeated, but two can stand back-to-back and conquer. Three are even better, for a triple-braided cord is not easily broken." Proverbs 3:5-6 instructs, "Trust in the Lord with all your heart; do not depend on your own understanding. Seek his will in all you do, and he will show you which path to take." God's guidance becomes clearer as we obey what He's revealed.

> ## ⚔ THE WARRIOR'S TOOLKIT
>
> Awareness isn't enough. You can see the battle clearly and still lose. Warriors need weapons.
>
> God has equipped you with three essential tools for reclaiming what the enemy has stolen:
>
> **The Identity Map** — for reclaiming your Purpose
> **The Truth Filter** — for reclaiming your Peace
> **The Passion Builder** — for reclaiming your Passion
>
> These aren't abstract concepts. They're practical instruments for the thousands of small skirmishes you face every day—each thought you entertain, each narrative you believe, each desire you pursue.
>
> Over the next three days, we'll take up each weapon in turn. But understand this now: the battle for your soul isn't won in a single dramatic moment. It's won in daily choices, with the right tools in hand.
>
> The armory is open. It's time to gear up.

Day 26
Finding Your God-Given Path

FRONTLINE FOCUS

In an age of endless options and constant FOMO (fear of missing out), many struggle with decision paralysis or jump between paths seeking the perfect life. Social media amplifies this anxiety by showcasing curated versions of others' journeys that seem more fulfilling than our own. God's promise of a known path offers profound relief from the exhausting search for the perfect life, replacing it with the peace of following His unique design for us.

WARRIOR REFLECTION

- **Understanding Truth:** How does Scripture describe the process of discovering and following God's path for our lives?
- **Heart Application:** Where in your journey have you been "knowing" without "doing"?

MEDITATION SCRIPTURE

"You will show me the way of life, granting me the joy of your presence and the pleasures of living with you forever." —Psalm 16:11

Prayer

Heavenly Father, thank You for having a specific path designed for my life that leads to fulfillment and purpose. Lord Jesus, You modeled perfect alignment with the Father's will, showing us how to walk in obedience and trust. Holy Spirit, illuminate the next steps You want me to take in following You. Integrate my purpose, peace, and passion so that every part of my life reflects Your design. I trust Your guidance even when the path isn't completely clear. Amen.

Battle Strategy

First Step

Identify one area where you know what God wants but haven't taken action. Today, move from knowing to doing by taking one concrete step of obedience in this area.

Going Deeper

Create a "life alignment assessment" examining how well your daily activities, relationships, and decisions align with your God-given purpose, peace, and passion. Identify one misalignment to address this week through specific changes.

Warrior Challenge

Develop a personal "rule of life" that integrates purpose, peace, and passion. Include daily, weekly, and monthly practices that keep these three elements in

Day 26
Finding Your God-Given Path

harmony. Share this plan with a spiritual mentor or friend who will help you implement and refine it over time.

NOTES:

DAY 27
DISCOVERING YOUR GOD GIVEN PURPOSE
EMBRACING YOUR TRUE IDENTITY
Voice of the Heart Reference: Chapter 27: Claiming Your Purpose

> *"Thank you for making me so wonderfully complex! Your workmanship is marvelous—how well I know it." —Psalm 139:14*

TODAY'S THEME

God's words to Jeremiah reveal a profound truth that applies to every believer: our purpose was established before our birth. God doesn't create randomly but with intentional design and specific calling. Your life isn't an accident or afterthought—it's the deliberate creation of a loving God who appointed you for particular good works.

BATTLEFIELD WISDOM

Finding our true purpose requires separating God's design from others' expectations. Family, culture, education, and society shape our understanding of who we should be. Some influences align with God's purposes while others pull us from our authentic identity.

Creating an "identity map" helps distinguish God's voice from competing influences. By examining what shaped your beliefs and evaluating which align with Scripture, you can separate truth from distortion. Ephesians 2:10 reminds us, "For we are God's masterpiece. He has created us anew in Christ Jesus, so we can do the good things he planned for us long ago." Your purpose isn't found in conforming to others' expectations but in embracing who God created you to be. Like David, who defeated Goliath with his own gifts rather than Saul's armor (1 Samuel 17), your greatest impact comes from your God-given identity.

FRONTLINE FOCUS

In a culture obsessed with self-definition and personal brand-building, the concept of discovering (rather than creating) your purpose offers profound freedom. Social media encourages constant identity reinvention based on trends and feedback, while God invites us to uncover the unchanging design He established before birth. This counter-cultural perspective shifts the question from "Who do I want to become?" to "Who has God already designed me to be?"

WARRIOR REFLECTION

- **Understanding Truth:** How does the biblical concept of God-given purpose differ from cultural messages about finding your purpose?

- **Heart Application:** What expectations or influences have shaped your understanding of your purpose that might be pulling you away from your authentic identity in Christ?

Day 27
Discovering Your God Given Purpose

MEDITATION SCRIPTURE

> "I knew you before I formed you in your mother's womb. Before you were born I set you apart and appointed you as my prophet to the nations."
> —Jeremiah 1:5

PRAYER

Heavenly Father, thank You for designing me with purpose and intention before I took my first breath. You are the master craftsman who shaped me for specific good works. Lord Jesus, You lived with perfect alignment to Your purpose, never swayed by others' expectations or demands. Holy Spirit, reveal the unique identity and calling God has placed within me. Help me discern between Your voice and the many other voices that try to define me. Amen.

BATTLE STRATEGY

FIRST STEP

Create a simple "identity map" today: List the key people, experiences, and messages that have shaped how you see yourself. For each influence, ask: "Does this align with how God describes me in Scripture?"

GOING DEEPER

Develop a "purpose discernment journal" where you record: 1) what energizes you, 2) what others affirm in you, 3) where you see fruit from your efforts, and 4) Scripture passages that speak to your identity. Review weekly for patterns that reveal God's design.

Warrior Challenge

Engage in a "purpose discovery retreat"—set aside a full day (or weekend if possible) for prayer, Scripture study, journaling, and reflection specifically focused on discerning God's unique design for your life. Include both solitude and conversation with trusted spiritual mentors.

NOTES:

Day 28
Peace That Stands on Truth

Filtering Out Deception
Voice of the Heart Reference: Chapter 28: Claiming Your Peace

> *"Don't worry about anything; instead, pray about everything. Tell God what you need, and thank him for all he has done. Then you will experience God's peace, which exceeds anything we can understand. His peace will guard your hearts and minds as you live in Christ Jesus."*
> —Philippians 4:6-7

Today's Theme

Paul describes God's peace as a guard protecting our hearts and minds—a spiritual security system that preserves our inner stability. This peace isn't just the absence of conflict but an active force that "transcends understanding," remaining steady even when circumstances seem to justify anxiety or fear.

Battlefield Wisdom

True peace is built on truth. When we align our thinking with God's reality, we experience stability through storms. Jesus connected truth with freedom: "And you will know the truth, and the truth will set you free." (John 8:32), releasing us from anxiety and confusion.

Developing a "truth filter" helps evaluate messages bombarding us. By testing information against reliable sources, recognizing manipulation, creating space for discernment, and connecting with truth-tellers, we protect our peace. Isaiah 26:3 promises, "You will keep in perfect peace all who trust in you, all whose thoughts are fixed on you!" This steadfast mind comes through anchoring in God's truth while filtering what shapes our perception.

FRONTLINE FOCUS

Today's digital environment has weaponized information, creating unprecedented challenges for maintaining mental and emotional peace. News algorithms prioritize outrage-inducing content, social media focuses on comparison and division, and advertising creates perpetual discontent. These forces combine to create what researchers call "continuous partial attention"—a state of constant low-grade anxiety that destroys inner peace and spiritual focus. Biblical peace practices have never been more counter-cultural or necessary.

WARRIOR REFLECTION

- **Understanding Truth:** How does Scripture describe the relationship between truth, trust, and peace?

- **Heart Application:** What specific messages or sources of information most often disturb your peace?

Day 28
Peace That Stands on Truth

MEDITATION SCRIPTURE

"And let the peace that comes from Christ rule in your hearts. For as members of one body you are called to live in peace. And always be thankful."
—Colossians 3:15

PRAYER

Heavenly Father, You are the unchanging rock upon which I can build a life of stability and peace. Lord Jesus, You offered peace not as the world gives, but a deeper tranquility that persists even in storms. Holy Spirit, You are the spirit of truth who guides us away from deception. Anchor my mind in Your truth when confusion surrounds me. Help me develop discernment that distinguishes reality from distortion. When noise and chaos threaten my clarity, guide me to the stillness where Your voice speaks. Amen.

BATTLE STRATEGY

FIRST STEP

Implement a "peace pause" practice today: Before reacting to troubling information, take 60 seconds to ask: "What do I know for certain about this situation?", "What might I be missing?", and "What does God's Word say that applies here?"

Going Deeper

Create a "peace preservation plan" identifying your top three peace-disturbers (specific information sources, thought patterns, or situations). For each one, develop a specific truth-based strategy for maintaining peace when exposed to these influences.

Warrior Challenge

Implement a monthly "digital truth fast"—a 24-hour period where you disconnect from news and social media while immersing yourself in Scripture, creation, and face-to-face relationships. Use this time to reset your peace baseline and recalibrate your truth filter.

NOTES:

_____
_____
_____
_____
_____
_____
_____
_____

Day 29
Fueling Your Spiritual Fire

Passion That Changes the World
Voice of the Heart Reference: Chapter 29: Claiming Your Passion

"You must love the LORD your God with all your heart, all your soul, all your strength, and all your mind." —Luke 10:27

Today's Theme

Paul's instruction to work "with all your heart" addresses the source of passionate living—seeing all we do as service to Christ rather than merely to people. This perspective transforms ordinary tasks into acts of worship and mundane responsibilities into meaningful ministry. When we recognize Jesus as the ultimate recipient of our efforts, everything changes.

Battlefield Wisdom

True passion flows from agape—selfless love seeking others' highest good. Unlike worldly passion that quickly fades, love-fueled passion sustains long-term impact. This explains why some achieve impressive things yet feel empty, while others serve in small ways with fulfillment.

Assessing your "flame gauge" identifies what fuels your spiritual fire. Jesus modeled this discernment, sometimes withdrawing to pray (Luke 5:16) and other times engaging intensely. Revelation 3:15-16 warns, "I know all the things you do, that you are neither hot nor cold. I wish that you were one or the other! But since you are like lukewarm water, neither hot nor cold, I will spit you out of my mouth!" Galatians 6:9 instructs, "So let's not get tired of doing what is good. At just the right time we will reap a harvest of blessing if we don't give up."

FRONTLINE FOCUS

In an age of clicktivism, shallow engagement, and chronic distraction, sustained passion for anything substantive has become increasingly rare. Digital notifications fragment our attention while algorithms feed us bite-sized emotional hits rather than deep engagement. Consumer culture encourages sampling many experiences rather than committed devotion to few. Against this backdrop, consistent, focused passion for God's kingdom stands out as a powerful witness to a distracted world.

WARRIOR REFLECTION

- **Understanding Truth:** What does Scripture teach about the relationship between love and sustained spiritual passion?
- **Heart Application:** What activities, relationships, or causes currently kindle your spiritual fire, and which ones tend to extinguish it?

Day 29
Fueling Your Spiritual Fire

MEDITATION SCRIPTURE

"Work willingly at whatever you do, as though you were working for the Lord rather than for people. Remember that the Lord will give you an inheritance as your reward, and that the Master you are serving is Christ." —Colossians 3:23-24

PRAYER

Heavenly Father, Your love burns with an intensity that never fades or grows cold. Lord Jesus, You demonstrated what wholehearted devotion looks like, pursuing the Father's will with undivided focus and commitment. Holy Spirit, You are the fire that ignites our hearts with divine passion. Reignite the flame of passion in my heart for the things that matter eternally. Help me discern which activities truly fuel my passion for Your kingdom. Amen.

BATTLE STRATEGY

FIRST STEP

Create a simple "flame gauge" today: List five regular activities or relationships in your life and rate each from 1-5 on how much they energize your spiritual passion. Choose one "level 4 or 5" activity to increase this week.

GOING DEEPER

Implement a weekly "passion protection" practice where you intentionally schedule at least one activity that reliably ignites your spiritual passion. Protect this time as you would any critical appointment, recognizing it as essential fuel for your spiritual life.

WARRIOR CHALLENGE

Identify the unique "holy passion" God has placed within you—a specific aspect of His kingdom that particularly stirs your heart. Develop a six-month engagement plan for this area, including learning, serving, and mobilizing others around this cause that connects your passion with God's purposes.

NOTES:

_____

_____

_____

_____

_____

_____

_____

_____

_____

Day 30
Shining as Light in the Darkness

Living Your Transformed Life
Voice of the Heart Reference:
Chapter 30: A Light at the End of the Road

"For God, who said, 'Let there be light in the darkness,' has made this light shine in our hearts so we could know the glory of God that is seen in the face of Jesus Christ." —2 Corinthians 4:6

Today's Theme

Jesus's declaration that "You are the light of the world" isn't a suggestion or goal but a statement of identity for His followers. When we align our purpose, peace, and passion with God's design, we naturally shine with a brightness that illuminates darkness around us. This light isn't something we create but something we reflect as we connect with the ultimate source of light—Jesus Himself.

Battlefield Wisdom

The integration of purpose, peace, and passion creates a powerful witness in a darkened world. When these three aspects of spiritual life work together, they produce something greater than the sum of their parts. Purpose gives direction, peace provides stability, and passion supplies energy. Together, they enable us to impact the world far beyond what any single element could accomplish alone.

This integration doesn't happen accidentally but through intentional practice. As 2 Corinthians 4:6 reminds us, "For God, who said, 'Let there be light in the darkness,' has made this light shine in our hearts so we could know the glory of God that is seen in the face of Jesus Christ." Our light comes from consistent connection with Christ through Scripture, prayer, worship, and obedience. Like the moon reflecting the sun's brilliance, we shine not with our own glory but with the reflected radiance of Jesus. As we walk in this light, we fulfill our calling as Paul describes in Philippians 2:15: "Live clean, innocent lives as children of God, shining like bright lights in a world full of crooked and perverse people."

FRONTLINE FOCUS

In a culture marked by increasing darkness—moral relativism, tribal division, nihilistic despair, and spiritual confusion—light becomes more visible and valuable. Digital spaces often amplify the worst aspects of human nature rather than the best. Against this backdrop, integrated followers of Christ who embody purpose, peace, and passion stand out with unmistakable distinctiveness, offering hope and direction to a disoriented world seeking meaning and authentic connection.

Day 30
Shining as Light in the Darkness

WARRIOR REFLECTION

- **Understanding Truth:** What does it mean to be "light" in a dark world according to Scripture?
- **Heart Application:** How integrated are your purpose, peace, and passion currently, and what would help these work together more effectively?

MEDITATION SCRIPTURE

"You are the light of the world—like a city on a hilltop that cannot be hidden. No one lights a lamp and then puts it under a basket. Instead, a lamp is placed on a stand, where it gives light to everyone in the house." —Matthew 5:14-15

PRAYER

Heavenly Father, You created light at the beginning of all things and continue to bring light into darkness through Your people. Lord Jesus, You declared Yourself the light of the world and called us to continue Your illuminating work. Holy Spirit, You shine God's light through us, making the invisible kingdom visible through transformed lives. Thank You for calling me to be light in this dark world. Integrate my purpose, peace, and passion so that my life reflects Your glory more clearly. Use my transformed life as a beacon that guides others toward Your love. Amen.

Battle Strategy

First Step

Choose one small but visible way to let your light shine today—perhaps through an unexpected act of kindness, speaking truth with grace in a difficult situation, or sharing how God has worked in your life.

Going Deeper

Create a "light assessment" by asking three trusted people: "Where do you see God's light shining most clearly in my life?" Use their feedback to identify your strongest areas of witness and the aspects of Christ's character you most clearly reflect.

Warrior Challenge

Develop an "integrated witness plan" that strategically aligns your purpose, peace, and passion to maximize your kingdom impact. Include specific ways you'll shine light in your family, workplace, church, and community. Review and refine this plan quarterly with a spiritual mentor or accountability partner.

NOTES:

Day 30
Shining as Light in the Darkness

Closing Prayer

Lord,

I come before You in awe of Your love and guidance, which has carried me through this journey. Thank You for revealing the battle I face and for equipping me with the truth to reclaim the life You intended for me. Thank You for showing me that I am more than a conqueror when I align with Your truth and follow Your voice.

I ask for Your continued presence as I step forward from this place. Help me carry what I've learned into every corner of my life. May I stand firm in my purpose, resting in Your truth and love. May I cultivate peace in my heart, no matter the storms I face. And may my passion, fueled by love, ignite change in the lives of those around me.

Lord, I surrender to You my hopes, fears, and dreams, knowing that Your plans for me are good. Transform me to live as salt and light, a representative of Your glory on earth.

May Your Spirit guide my steps, strengthen my resolve, and remind me that I am never alone in this battle. I pray that through this journey, I not only reclaim my life but inspire others to do the same—leading hearts back to You.

In Jesus' name, Amen.

About the Author
A Journey in Pursuit of Purpose, Peace, and Passion

Greg Pai's *Voice of the Heart* franchise is the culmination of a lifelong journey to understand the invisible forces that shape our lives. Drawing upon diverse experiences across multiple industries including finance, technology, media, entertainment, and consulting, Greg recognized a common thread: the struggle to maintain purpose, peace, and passion amid a world that often seems designed to undermine them.

Everything changed on February 12, 2012, when Greg and his wife Lynn came to faith together at Hawthorne Gospel Church in New Jersey. Within months, Greg joined the worship team, and soon after, he and Lynn felt called to bring their business skills and resources to the unreached world through missions—traveling to East and North Africa, the Middle East, and Southeast Asia often in partnership with major missions organizations.

This journey planted the seeds for the Voice of the Heart collection. Greg's desire is not to tell others what to believe, but to share what God has done in his life and to invite others—regardless of background or belief—to explore the deeper questions we all carry. His approach is rooted in love and respect, encouraging each person to pursue their own journey toward truth and the filling of the void that exists within us all.

Greg shares his life with Lynn, his wife of over 25 years, their four children, and four beloved furry companions.

CONTINUE THE JOURNEY

Each day in this devotional references chapters from Voice of the Heart—the complete guide to understanding the invisible forces that shape your life and the path to reclaiming your true identity in Christ.

VOICE OF THE HEART: THE BATTLE FOR YOUR PURPOSE, PEACE, AND PASSION

The full exploration of the systems, strategies, and scriptural truths that set you free.

VOICE OF THE HEART: ESSENTIAL EDITION

A condensed journey for those ready to begin.

**Both available at Amazon,
Barnes & Noble, and booksellers worldwide.**

www.ingramcontent.com/pod-product-compliance
Lightning Source LLC
Chambersburg PA
CBHW071952070426
42453CB00012BA/2141